A Theological Response to Street Children

Christian Heritage Rediscovered

The Series, as the name suggests, is meant to focus on Christian Faith & Living vis-à-vis topics like Literature & Poetry, Indigenous Philosophizing, Ethical response towards Agriculture, Health & Healing, Science & Technology, Ecofeminist Theology, Sociological approach towards Human Rights, Law & Politics, Arts, History of Ideas, Ancient Civilizations, Cultural Contiguity, Religious Cosmologies & Mysticism, Footsteps of famous Theologians, World Peace & Harmony, Global Capitalism, Network Marketing, Cybertheology, Population & Demographics, Epigraphic Studies, Contextualized Education, and many others. We welcome a Mss. on any topic/s mentioned, whether they are original works, scholarly monographs, collections of conference papers, revised dissertations, or translations of historical documents. Through the Series we, the Publishers, are striving to put forward published works that may help Institutions, Academic Bodies, Researchers, Scholars and the World at large in furthering their respective knowledge and understanding on the concerned subject. We welcome your comments on our efforts and further suggestions on how we can foster the upcoming thoughtful theologically grounded books.

Christian Heritage Rediscovered - 19

A Theological Response to Street Children

An Empirical Study

Potana Venkateswara Rao

CWI

Christian World Imprints™

First Published in 2015 by

Christian World Imprints™
Christian Publishing & Books from India
H-12 Bali Nagar, **New Delhi-110015**
info@christianworldimprints.com
www.ChristianWorldImprints.com
Phone: +91 11 25465925

ISBN-13: 978-93-5148-053-2 (HB) ISBN-10: 93-5148-053-4 (HB)
ISBN-13: 978-93-5148-057-0 (PB) ISBN-10: 93-5148-057-7 (PB)

Cataloging in Publication Data--DK
Courtesy: D.K. Agencies (P) Ltd. <docinfo@dkagencies.com>

Venkateswara Rao, Potana, 1974- **author**.
A theological response to street children : an empirical study / Potana Venkateswara Rao.
pages cm. -- (Christian heritage rediscovered ; 19)
Includes index.
ISBN 9789351480532 (HB)
ISBN 9789351480570 (PB)

1. Street children--Rehabilitation--India--Vijayawāda. 2. Children--Religious aspects--Christianity. I. Title. II. Series: Christian heritage rediscovered ; 19.

DDC 233 23

Printed at Chawla Offset Printers

What Others Say!

The good news that Potana presents in these pages is that, like children everywhere, street children are very responsive to loving actions. God is ready to perform miracles of transformation in their lives. Potana's many case studies of transformed street children will be an encouragement to any one making a sincere attempt to minister to the needs of children in India or in any other nation. Sri Potana helps us to understand the biblical call to minister to street children. His academic overview of the challenge presented by street children, and his case studies of street children trying to survive in the Indian city of Vijayawada, reveal a compelling opportunity for followers of Jesus to show love to those who are most dear to the heart of God.

-David E. Stravers
C.E.O., Mission India

This book will undoubtedly prove to be a valuable asset in discovering the conditions, problems and struggles children face in today's world. I am confident that anyone who reads this book will understand the issues involved and will be moved to act towards the betterment of society and the country itself.

-Prem Kumar Kothapalli
Software Engineer, TCS, New Jersey, USA

Potana's work on street children is well-researched, compassionate, and groundbreaking. He carefully ties in the problem of street children around the world, the compassionate acts already done by Christians, and urges them not to forget those already born who cannot ask for help.

-Caroline P Misarski
Announcer, WIHS Radio, Middletown, CT, USA

In this book, my friend Venkat has systematically researched, carefully analyzed and intentionally visualized the plight of street children in India, and compassionately casts a stern call before its readers to take up the task more seriously. It is very informative and useful to those who have a vision to reach out to the excluded, underprivileged and exploited street children in India.

-Rev. Manohar James
President, Redeem India, Inc.
www.redeemindia.org

Dedicated

To my dear wife Rita Rao
&
my lovely children Sophia,
Lydia & Ashish Vidwan Rao
who is behind me in every success.

The Book

This book is meant to be a squeaky wheel to bring up the issue of street children evaluating their present condition globally as well as locally. This well-explored presentation focuses on the subject which otherwise was always neglected within the social sciences especially in theological studies. Presently, several Social Work Agencies & NGOs are working to rehabilitate these street children, but still this social disease needs serious attention by the public at large and especially by the Christian community.

During the Biblical times 'street children' was not a serious issue as it is now, but there are instances that can help us to understand God's concern for the poor and rejected people on the streets, which includes children also. The Bible has much to say on the provision and protection of the children. Contrary to the Bible sayings, these runaway kids get involved in social crimes as well as sexual abuse and consequently develop HIV infection. The missiological research on children proves that this is the right age to help them to know God who can liberate them from all the oppressive structures.

The Author carefully ties in the problem of street children around the world with the humane acts already done by Christians. But, he is also concerned with the increasing number of street children especially in India. This well-researched, compassionate, and groundbreaking book is for those who have a real concern for these special gifts of God.

The Author

Sri Potana Venkateswara Rao, also known as Bhakta Potana, hails from Andhra Pradesh, India. His academic credentials include a Bachelor's degree in English literature from Acharya Nagarjuna University; a Masters degree in social work from the same university; a Master's degree in Religion & Philosophy from Madurai Kamaraj University; a Master of Divinity degree from GFA Seminary, Tiruvalla, Kerala, India; and a Master of Theology degree from Union Biblical Seminary, Pune. At present, he is conducting research for Ph.D. with the University of Mysore through the South Asia Institute of Advanced Christian Studies, Bangalore. Sri Potana lives in Bangalore with his wife Rita and their three children Sophia, Lydia & Ashish Vidwan Rao.

For the past few years, Sri Potana has been teaching God's word to university students in India. His three years (1993-1996) as a student leader and eleven years (2000-2011) as a full time staff for the Union of Evangelical Students of India (UESI) opened opportunities for him to impact college and university students in both South and North India. He is not only an academician but he is a man on the mission field who is down to earth.

Potana Venkateswara Rao
SAIACS Campus, Near Ayyappa Temple
Dodda Gubbi Cross Road, Kothanur Post
Bangalore-560077
+91-7899124389
pothanav@gmail.com

Foreword

The vast majority of people hanker after their childhood. They long to be transported back to a time where they saw the world differently, to add color to life, to experience the love and care of parents; a time where they had no job and no responsibilities. For them, childhood was a beautiful and wonderful stage of life and one they miss. But, there are too many who miss the innocence and wonder of childhood and are forced into adulthood far too prematurely. We have come across such children every day and everywhere. The reactions of people to these children are varied. Some thank God that they did not have a life such as this; some gets irritated by these children; while others act as if they don't belong to this world. There are a very few who give them any thought. Bhakta Potana, the author of this book, is among the few.

I have known Potana since 1993. Even as a student he knew the value of life and its purpose in this world. For this reason, I am not surprised that his heart turned towards the plight of the "little buddies." It is my privilege and honour to write a foreword to this book.

In this book, Potana has compacted all his research work among street children and has narrated their life tragedies such as you have most likely never heard before. I am confident that your perspective towards street children will change after reading this book. The next time you look at them it will be with helpful and prayerful eyes. God said that we are the light of the world, so let us shine our light on those withering little buds and make their life shine brighter.

Mr. Nireekshan Rao
Teacher, Khammam, India

Preface

They don't wake up under the covers.
They don't taste breakfast in the morning.
They don't play in the park with other boys and girls.
There was no bread, just some bitter tea, a bitter life, burning the tongue and the dreams.
There was no paper, There was no school, There was no future, Boys and Girls of the No.
In their hands, an infinite sadness . . .
The hands of these little ones are more adult than their eyes.... [1]

The phenomenon of 'street children' is a global and urban issue that needs serious attention. Regrettably however, the topic of street-children was a neglected one within the social sciences and especially in theological and missiological studies. Bryant L. Myers rightly observed, "Understanding the situation of children and youth in the world is a significant blind spot in Christian mission."[2] In our Indian context, Christian missions have more awareness of and focus on the condition of tribals and dalits and less on the pressing urban

1 Lima Soares and Zena de, "Children: A Permanent Challenge for the Churches," *International Review of Mission* 85, no. 338 (July 1996), 429.

2 Bryant Myers, "State of the World's Children: Critical Challenge to Christian Mission," *International Bulletin of Missionary Research* 18, no. 3 (July 1, 1994), 98.

issue of street children. The distressing thing is that these runaway children soon get involved with middle men/women who exploit them by forcing them into begging, bonded labor and the sex trade. This is an alarming and serious social problem in India and needs to be studied from a missiological perspective in order to help this community feel a part of society as a whole. This book presents the condition and the context of the street children; tries to explain why and how street children are excluded; and progresses to address the issue of how they can be included into society, the family, and the church. There are several non-governmental organizations (NGOs) and a few Christian organizations that are working to rehabilitate these street children but still the issue needs serious attention as to the research and innovative methods needed to reach them.

Why are street children important? Are they important in the kingdom of God? Do we have a mission for them? What is the Christian response to them? These are some of the questions that we need to ask ourselves in order to understand them. The number of street children is growing day by day because of the tremendous growth of urbanization, worldwide economic down fall, unemployment, and the breakdown of the family system. There are about 100 million street children in the world today who are excluded from the privileges and rights to which all children are entitled. In fact, "India has the greatest number of street children" in the world.[3] As per R. Agarwal's estimation, the number of street children in India is 20 million, i.e., approximately 7% of the total child population of the world.[4] The total of all the street children in India is more than half of the population of Canada and four times bigger than the population of New Zealand.

The increase of street children day by day in our urban context and their struggle for existence raises the question, "how do street children survive and how can we build a nation when they are

3 "United Nations Development Programme (UNDP)" (Oxford University Press, New York, 1993), 24, http://hdr.undp.org/en/media/hdr_1993_en_chap2.pdf.

4 R. Agrawal, *Streetchildren: A Socio-Psychological Study* (Shipra Publications, 1999), 28.

exploited in different ways."[5] In order to bring about improvement in our country, we need to protect our children from danger and traps.

Street children are emotionally scarred and disturbed because these they are abandoned and excluded by society. These children are often "exposed more to dogs than to kindness."[6] Since the street children face rejection, they are not open to speak and express their feelings. These children are usually not productive because of their disturbed condition due to various reasons, therefore they feel lonely and rejected and live with low self-esteem, all of which leads them to destructive habits. Our country's asset, 'Our Children', is under threat. Therefore concentrating on children, especially street children, is the need of the hour in our Indian context.

As a Bhakta of Christ, I have a great respect and love for India. My desire and love for street kids motivated me to do this research which affected me to pray and do something for them. I am sure that this book will open your eyes to see the need on the streets.

I pray that this book will be a great blessing to all those who read and reflect on it. May the Lord give you a compassionate heart for the needy world.

09/02/2014

Bhakta Potana
Bangalore

---

5 Shanchobeni Yanthan and Pelekhono Zinyu, "Street Children and Christian Response," in *Children At Risk: Issues and Challenges* (Bangalore: ISPCK, 2009), 267.

6 John Boswell, *The Kindness of Strangers: The Abandonment of Children in Western Europe from Late Antiquity to the Renaissance* (University of Chicago Press, 1988), 172.

Acknowledgements

This book in its original form was my dissertation submitted to the Acharya Nagarjuna University, in partial fulfillment of the requirement for the degree of Master of Arts in Social Work in 2011. So, first of all I want to thank the university for granting me permission to publish my thesis. Also, I am responsible for the changed title, contents and the opinions expressed in it with all the due permissions required. I am grateful to my mentor Professor Trimurthi Rao, Dept. of Sociology and Social Work, who guided me in a way that I could explore the reality of street kids in India. He gave his timely guidance and helped me in finishing my research work.

I am thankful to Mrs. G. M. Priscilla who is the manager of Vijayawada Street Children Project, World Vision of India, Vijayawada. My heartfelt thanks go to Mr. Yesurathnam who helped me in several ways to finish this project. I am grateful to Mrs. Malathi Benjamin for her professional editing of the text. Also, I owe thanks to the World Vision staff Mr. Divakar, Mr. Subba Rao, Mrs. Mary and volunteers Mrs. Florence, Mrs. Dhanalakshmi, Mrs. Santhi, and Mr. Anand who helped me in interacting with the street children in the field to get case studies. Their support is noteworthy and I appreciate their service rendered to me.

Contents

Chapter 1

Research, Rationale and Methodology

Introduction

The phenomenon of runaway children is a growing one in the global context and especially in India. Child labor, sexual abuse, prostitution, child trafficking, HIV / AIDS, malnutrition, illiteracy, chronic illness, urban migration, homelessness, addiction, gender discrimination, police abuse, injustice, violent behavior, torture, murder, suicide, and serious crimes of every variety –these social issues are rampant among children of the street. It is a sad truth that at least 40,000 children in a population of 1.3 million are identified at one point of time as street children, according to municipal statistics. Vasavya Mahila Mandali, a non-governmental organization, has undertaken programs to rehabilitate these street children who bring with them unique problems. Sixty percent of these children keep migrating from town to town. Rehabilitation by institutionalizing them or returning them to their respective families is not feasible because of their constant movement.[7] Many of these children have run away from home because they were beaten or sexually abused. Tragically, their homelessness can lead to further abuse through exploitative child labor and prostitution.

Not only does abuse rob runaway children of their material security, it also leaves them emotionally scarred. These children are abandoned by society.[8] Boswell John writes, "Concerning abandoned children: there is general complaint that they are nowadays exposed more to dogs than to kindness."[9] Many of the abused children living in cities are traumatized and some refuse to speak for months. To exacerbate matters, the children often feel guilty and blame themselves for their mistreatment. Such damage can take years to recover from even in the most loving of environments. It is imperative that the state and civil society immediately focus and give attention to the rehabilitation of street children.

Biblical Basis

The Bible often expresses God's deep concern for the poorest and most powerless members of human society. In the Old Testament, God's people are commanded to defend the aliens and the orphans, two groups most likely to suffer abuse in the societies of the ancient Near East. In the New Testament Jesus loves the poor, and says about children, "Of such is the kingdom of God…Unless you become like a little child, you cannot enter the kingdom." Fast forwarding the application of these statements to the 21st century, it is hard to imagine a group more deserving of the loving attention of God's people than street children.

The Bible clearly affirms that all children are a special gift from God (Psalm 127:3). God gives value to life and its progress because human beings are created in the image of God (Gen 1:26-27). Hence, God demands we give full respect, dignity and value to every human being irrespective of whether they live in a palace or on the streets. On the issue of the dignity of a child, Frampton F. Fox states that, "children should be valued not based on what they might do for us in the future, but rather recognized as having value that is intrinsic, given by God."[10] We should concentrate on children, not with the ulterior motive of having them serve us in church or in society but as an obligation from God. Indeed God used children as leaders to fulfill His great purposes and the Old Testament records that God is concerned about children.

During the Biblical times 'street children' may not have been a serious issue as it is now, but there are instances that can help us understand God's concern for the poor and rejected people on the streets, including children. The Bible has much to say on provision and protection of children. God's instructions on raising children (Deut. 11:19, Eph. 6:4, Prov. 22:6), if followed, would prevent children from running away from home. God has a special concern for the fatherless and the alien (Deut. 10:18). Street children are homeless aliens living on the streets. A huge numbers of them overflow to the streets because they are orphans or semi-orphans. The Old Testament concept of "kinsman-redeemer" (Ruth 3:9) demands that we redeem these children from the streets. Therefore, we have a mandate to prevent children from running away and to provide for and protect them.

Cain ran away from his parents with guilt and shame, but God found this run away murderer and rehabilitated him with His protection. "Then the Lord put a mark on Cain so that no one who found him would kill him" (Genesis 4:14-16). When Hagar's little boy was crying for survival at one of the bushes near the road side, "God heard the boy crying" (Genesis 21: 17). In fact, God said, "Lift the boy up and take him by the hand, for I will make him into a great nation" (Genesis 21:18). As a semi orphan, Ishmael might have gone through the pain of rejection and "may be, Ishmael was a street kid trying to earn food for his mother by hunting and selling animals."[11] God found this street child and rehabilitated him along with his mother, which helps us understand God's concern for the street children in our Indian cities. In fact God is in the mission of rehabilitating rejected, exploited, oppressed, harassed and helpless children. He calls the church to engage in this mission to street children.

The heroes of the Bible such as Jacob, Joseph and Moses journeyed on the streets hoping for love, acceptance, security and settlement. Joseph's bitter experience with his half-brothers and bonded labor in Egypt reveal the pain, struggle and suffering of today's street child in Indian cities. However, he was rehabilitated by God through the provision of a skilled training and a well-paid and position of honor and trust in the foreign land of Egypt, all in order to fulfill His plans and purposes. Apostle Paul sent back the runaway slave Onesimus to his master with the aim of including him in the Christian fellowship we call "the Church" (Philemon 1). Jesus was the defender of the poor, rejected, oppressed, harassed and helpless. He welcomed little children into His presence. It is my conviction that Jesus' Nazareth manifesto (Luke 4:17-19) includes street children in His redemptive mission. Therefore, the church has an obligation to respond to street children with compassion and care.

Significance of the Study

This study delves into the plight of street children and also evaluates the present condition of street children globally as well as locally. This study focuses on the global scenario with an in-depth attention to the Indian context, with particular reference to the city of Vijayawada. There are several social work agencies and NGOs that are working to rehabilitate these street children, but still the issue needs serious attention, research and innovative projects.

A matter of significance is that India is one of the younger countries in the world to make a tremendous impact in the field of economy, science and technology. In order to improve our country we need to protect our children from dangers and we should allow and encourage our young children to climb the ladder of success. A. P. J. Abdul Kalam states that "there is likely to be a large population of young people with aspirations of better lifestyle" by the year 2020.[12] In fact, if we observe the Indian population, "More than 50% of the population is less than 25 years of age and strong growth is expected to continue in this age bracket."[13] These young people's potential needs to be tapped from their childhood days otherwise we may not see strong young crowds in the country. This study is an attempt to understand the whole issue of "street children" and to help the NGOs to focus on rehabilitating them so that our nation may continue to progress.

Areas of Study

Location: The researcher selected Vijayawada for his field study. There are several reasons for this but the major reason is that the researcher selected the NGO, Vijayawada Street Children Project of World Vision, located in this city, which has had a tremendous impact on the issue.

Vijayawada Street Children Project, World Vision of India

World Vision is a Christian relief and development agency helping children and their communities towards a wholesome future filled with hope, dignity, justice and peace. Reaching out to the poorest of the poor in India without respect to caste, creed, race or religion, World Vision works through partnerships to bring about lasting change and build our nation. Internationally, World Vision emerged out of a faithful expression of God's love by Robert Pierce, a war correspondent during the Korean War in 1947.

World Vision's work in India began in 1962, in a small way in Calcutta. Today, its staff works in close to 5,000 communities, touching the lives of more than 24 million people in India. World Vision is a registered society under the Tamilnadu Societies Act 1975, with its National Office in Chennai. It is an independent entity within our country with a distinct national identity. An active Indian Board of Directors governs World Vision. World Vision India is a member of the international partnership of World Vision, which works in roughly 100 countries. World Vision has consultative status with UNESCO as well as official relations with key UN agencies including UNICEF, WHO, UNHCR and ILO.

Children are the focus of World Vision's work. It works together with the communities, families and children in their journey toward development. It does this by working with the communities to help them reach the basic standards of physical, intellectual, socio-economic and moral well-being. World Vision facilitates the formation and growth of community-based organizations, which are able to identify the problems faced by the community, especially children, and work with them to find solutions. This is its strategy for sustainable development. World Vision also responds to disasters due to natural calamities in the country. It has responded to every major disaster, starting from the cyclone in Machilipatnam, Andhra Pradesh in 1977 to the floods in Bihar and Uttar Pradesh. World Vision stays in the disaster-struck area until the community is back on its feet.

World Vision's work in India is spread over 24 states across the country. Today its staff works in close to 5,000 communities, touching the lives of a more than 24 million people, with 1,65,000 children directly benefiting through child sponsorship. 93 lakh children are benefited through various other programs of World Vision around the country through the dedicated work of its staff in India.

World Vision works with communities, families and children in their journey towards self-sufficiency. Its unique way of doing this is through integrated development programs that bring about lasting change in the communities. World Vision works in communities through 106 Area Development Programs (ADPs). Each ADP touches the lives of over 20,000 to 1,000,000 people.

World Vision's Street Children Project

World Vision started its street children in November 2008 at Vijayawada. Although it is an international organization which primarily caters to community developmental projects its street children project was initiated to empower runaway children. World Vision has staff that is assigned to bus stations, railway stations and signal points whose job it is to trace street children, especially those who have run away from their homes. Those children are brought to the drop-in center where information about them is gathered and where they are given professional counseling in a secure environment. Mostly the organization attempts to return the child to the safety of his or her parents or other concerned person. Those who don't reveal their family history and those who do not want to go back to their home are handed over to existing Children's Homes in the city.

Elaboration of the Problem

Many of the street children who have run away from home have done so because they were beaten or sexually abused. They often face sexual harassment at the hands of adults and their peers. Girls are easily exploited and are gradually introduced into prostitution. Sexually abused children are prone to sexually transmitted diseases such as HIV/AIDS. In damning statistics, a government study has found that a vast majority of street children face sexual abuse in India, home to the world's largest number of destitute children. According to a study conducted by the Ministry of Women and Child Development, the overall incidence of physical abuse among street children was 66.8 per cent. The majority of the street children facing physical abuse are in the age group of 5-12 years. Around 55 per cent of the street children reported having suffered sexual abuse.[14]

Children may end up on the streets for several reasons: They may have no choice – they are abandoned, orphaned, or disowned by their parents; They may choose to live in the streets because of mistreatment or neglect or because their homes do not or cannot provide them with basic necessities; Many children also work in the streets because their earnings are needed by their families. But, homes and families are part of the larger society and the underlying reasons for the poverty or breakdown of homes and families may be social, economic, political or environmental or any combination of these. This study attempts to understand this societal problem and to give some suggestions and recommendations to lessen the problem in the society, particularly in the city of Vijayawada.

Objectives of the Study

1. The main objective of this study is to gain a comprehensive understanding on the subject of "Street Children" through field experience so that the researcher may contribute something to these underprivileged children.
2. To understand the definitions, issues and classifications of street children in order to have a thorough understanding of the problems and implications relating to street children.
3. To study the existing response to the street children from government and Non-governmental organizations and to understand the condition and struggles of street children in Vijayawada and the rehabilitation work that is being done for them by different agencies.
4. To collect first hand data from the "Street Children Project" from World Vision, to have field experience, and to ascertain rational findings from the data and to help the concerned NGOs improve their service to these street children.

5. To enlighten society on this issue so the street children may be taken care of by the public.

Limitations

This research is limited to the City of Vijayawada. In reality, however, the plight of street children is an international issue and it has great attention in third world countries and especially in our country, India. World Vision India has a huge network in India because it has been working in all the states for many decades. The research is limited to the city of Vijayawada and it is not a comparative study of other social work agencies and NGOs. There is not much literature on street children. Although there are a few books written on street children, this researcher found little relevant literature in the context of rehabilitating street children in Andhra Pradesh. This is one of the major limitations in reviewing the literature.

Methodology

This study comprises empirical research. Primary and secondary sources were used in this research. Sources from the internet, library books and a few journals were extensively used to create a theoretical framework. A set of structured and well-prepared participant observation, group discussion, and personal interviews was used to get accurate information from the field and some documents from the World Vision offices were collected and used in the presentation of the data.

Sampling

The researcher strategically selected samples with the help of World Vision staff from the field as well as from its office.

Runaway children interviewed	14
World vision staff interviewed	6
Participant observations (Child homes)	5
Informal observations (Streets & slums)	5
Total	**30**

Data Collection

Initially the researcher asked one of the World Vision staff members to get permission from the organization to enable collection of data. It took some time for the researcher to get such permission from their central office located in Chennai. A pilot interview was conducted with one of the office staff and the researcher started collecting the data by structured interviews, planned participant observations, and informal observations from the field.

The researcher travelled to different places in the city of Vijayawada and made frequent visits to bus stands, railway stations, cinemas, junctions, a few slums, a few child care centers and street children rehabilitation centers, run by different NGOs. During these visits and travels the researcher noted all the data without fail in his laptop as well as in his note book. The drop-in center of World Vision was the main source for interviews from the runaway children. Another primary source was World Vision's documents. A few documents were collected from the World Vision office and all sources are faithfully acknowledged in the foot notes.

Data Processing

The collected data was studied and tabulated systematically. Systematic and logical tables and figures were organized from the tabulation of the data. Valuable statements and information from the interviews were added to interpret the tables and figures.

Library Research

The library research method was used to understand what people have written in connection with the researcher's topic and to create a theoretical framework with which the field data could be analyzed in the light of what people have already written on this subject. Online journals from the internet and books related to this title were identified in the library.

Outline of the Research

Chapter One deals with the introduction of the study, which includes the problem statement and related explanation, the objectives of the study, definitions, limitations, and a detailed description of the research methodology. Chapters Two, Three, and Four cover the review of the literature related to the research topic. The Fifth chapter presents case studies, Data Collection, and Data Analysis. The final chapter presents the major findings and conclusions that were derived from the interpretation of the data and makes recommendations.

Chapter 2

Definitions, Issues and Classifications

Introduction

A street child is a term used to refer children who live on the streets of a city, deprived of family care and protection. Most children on the streets are between the ages of about 5 and 17 years old, and their population between different cities is varied.

Street children live in junk boxes, parks or on the street itself. A great deal has been written defining street children, but the primary difficulty is that there are no precise categories, but rather a continuum, ranging from children who spend some time in the streets and sleep in a house with ill-prepared adults, to those who live entirely in the streets and have no adult supervision or care. This project is a study on the subject aimed at gaining a more comprehensive understanding of the issues involved in order to educate the public so that the readers may be inspired to get involved in rehabilitating street kids. A widely accepted set of definitions, commonly attributed to Amnesty International, divides street children into two main categories:

Children on the street are those engaged in some kind of economic activity ranging from begging to selling things. Most go home at the end of the day and contribute their earnings to their family. They may be attending school and retain a sense of belonging to a family. Because of the economic fragility of the family, these children may eventually opt for a permanent life on the streets.

Children of the street actually live on the street (or outside of a normal family environment). Family ties may exist but are tenuous and are maintained only casually or occasionally.[15]

Street children exist in many major cities, especially in developing countries, and may be subject to abuse, neglect, exploitation, or even, in extreme cases, murder by "cleanup squads" hired by local businesses or police.[16]

In Latin America, and in parts of Asia a common reason for children finding themselves on the street is abandonment by poor families unable to feed all their children. In Africa, an increasingly common cause is the death of the parents, often of AIDS, or the illness rendering them unable to care for their children.

In Western societies such children are termed "homeless children". According to the Sunnykids children charity of Australia, homelessness in Western societies tends to fall into three categories: Primary (rough sleeping, literally living on the streets); Secondary (moving from place to place, utilizing support such as staying with friends, living in a homeless shelter; and Tertiary (those known as "at risk" of homelessness such as children that have a home which they are under significant risk of losing or which they may be unsafe in).

Definition

The question of how to define a street child has generated much discussion that is usefully summarized by Sarah Thomas de Benítez in, "The State of the World's Street Children: Violence."

'Street children' is increasingly recognized by sociologists and anthropologists to be a socially constructed category that in reality does not form a clearly defined, homogeneous population or phenomenon. 'Street children' covers children in such a wide variety of circumstances and characteristics that policy-makers and service providers find it difficult to describe and target them. Upon peeling away the 'street children' label, individual girls and boys of all ages are found living and working in public spaces, visible in the great majority of the world's urban centers.

The definition of 'street children' is contested, but many practitioners and policymakers use UNICEF's concept of boys and girls aged under 18 for whom 'the street' (including unoccupied dwellings and wasteland) has become home and/or their source of livelihood, and who are inadequately protected or supervised.[17]

Names

Street Children is a widely used term in the English language and has analogues in other languages such as French (les enfants des rues), Spanish (niños de la calle), Portuguese (meninos da rua), Hungarian (utcagyerekek), Romanian (străzii) and German (Straßenkinder). The term Street Kids is also commonly employed although it is considered pejorative.[18] In other languages children who live and/or work in the streets are known by many names. Some examples are listed below:[19]

- "huelepegas" (glue sniffers) in Nicaragua
- "chemos" (glue sniffers) in Mexico
- "gamín" (from French gamin, kid)
- "chinches" (bed bugs) in Colombia
- "pivetes" (little criminals/marginals) in Rio de Janeiro
- "pájaro frutero" (fruit bird) and "pirañitas" (little piranhas) in Peru
- "polillas" (moths) in Bolivia
- "resistoleros" (glue sniffers; Resistol is a major brand) in Honduras
- "scugnizzi" (spinning tops) in Naples
- "беспризорники" - besprizorniki (those without supervision) in Russia
- "batang lansangan"/"batang kalye" (street child), "palaboy" (waif or vagrant, also a general term applied to homeless people), or "rugby boys" in the Philippines (glue sniffers; rugby being a brand of wood glue)
- "Bụi Đời" (the dust of life) in Vietnam

- "saligoma" (dirty kid, from French Sale gamin) in Rwanda
- "poussins" (chicks), "moustiques" (mosquitos) in Cameroon
- "balados" (wanderers) in the Democratic Republic of the Congo and the Congo Republic.

The term Street Arab came to the fore in the mid-19th century, first appearing in 1848, according to the OED.[20] Horatio Alger's book Tattered Tom or, The Story of a Street Arab (1871) is an early example; it is about a homeless girl living by her wits on the streets of New York. Charles Dickens likewise propagated its early use in 1855 but in a more clearly derogatory sense when he declared "a wretched, ragged, untaught street Arab boy is ugly."[21] Jacob Riis addresses street children in New York as "The Street Arab."[22]

The Victorian association of street children with Arabs was most likely caused by the nomadic tradition of Arabs who were wanderers; the 19th century notion that non-Europeans from less civilized cultures were like children; European and American travelers who saw many "street children" in Arab countries during the period; and a xenophobic tendency to scapegoat social problems. The term has fallen out of favor.

Issues of the Street & Working Children

The issues and needs of children living and working on city streets have attracted widespread international and national attention. There is no doubt that the most effective response to this is prevention through the general support of families in poverty; creating a broad-based awareness among parents and society; and addressing the factors underlying family disintegration that propel children into a life on the streets. In addition, to keep families intact so that they fulfill their responsibilities towards their children, other preventive measures to be considered are employment for adults, support in times of crisis, strong childcare programs, relevant schooling and efforts to address the root of domestic violence

At the same time, the children already on the streets cannot be ignored, and their rights must be vigorously defended. They need psychological support, relationships, and a role in society along with other basic needs related to their survival: security and protection, food, money, shelter, clothes, healthcare, education, etc. Like all other children, they have the right to live in dignity, to health and education, to protection from abuse, exploitation, violence, and to voice their own feelings and sufferings (Articles 2 and 3 of the U.N. Convention on the Rights of the Child). While developing strategies for the rehabilitation of the street children, one must understand their case histories and the assessment of their situation. Reasons for being on the street vary with each child. The sense of freedom may be intensely important to many of these children. Depriving them of this freedom may exacerbate matters, especially when a child has strong ties to a group of peers. This involves establishing a relationship of trust with them and providing them with a safe and supportive atmosphere. Institutionalization is definitely not the solution. Strategy has to be integrated with other services on the street.

The reality of child labor is one of the major concerns facing the international community. There are determined efforts to respond to the issues and at the same time arrive at progressive solutions. The Convention on the Rights of the Child contains a number of provisions pertaining to children's work, which together provide a framework for policy and action. The Convention requires that children be protected from all exploitative and hazardous work, and from work that interferes with their education and full development. To ensure this the State is required to set a minimum age for employment and regulate working conditions (Article 32). The Convention also recognizes the right of children to the means for survival (Article 6). The uncomfortable reality in India is that children's work is often the only apparent means to their survival. In the context of widespread poverty and the absence of a welfare system that guarantees a livelihood for children and their families, work remains the most viable option for many children. The response from the state and society must offer them protection as well as tackle the problems that make their work a necessity. The Convention calls to authorities to support parents in their effort to ensure their children's optimal development and adequate standard of living (Articles 18, 27). The Convention also guarantees access to free, relevant, high quality education, which is a critical element in resolving the issue of child labor. While governments and civil societies progress towards eradicating inappropriate child labor and the presence of street children, they must address their concerns, and ensure their access to education, a high quality of healthcare, rest and leisure, and acceptable working conditions (Articles 12, 24, 28, 31, 32 of the Rights of the Child).

Children in Difficult Circumstances - Concept and Definition

Children in difficult circumstances include both the street children and children working in inappropriate work processes and situations. The term 'child labor' is generally used to refer to, "any work by children (under 14 years of age in India) that interferes with their full physical and mental development, the opportunities for a desirable minimum of education, and the need for recreation."[23]

In reality, children do a variety of work in widely divergent conditions. At one end of the continuum, such work is destructive and/or exploitative. At the other end, the work may be beneficial, providing or enhancing a child's physical, mental, spiritual, moral or social development without interfering with schooling, recreation and rest.

Fyfe attempts to provide a distinction by differentiating between "Child Work" and "Child Labor." Child work is considered permissible, while child labor is prohibitive. According to the U.N. Convention on the Rights of the Child (Article 32), "State parties recognize the right of the child to be protected from economic exploitation and from performing any work that is likely to be hazardous or to be harmful to the child's education, or to be harmful to the child's health or physical, mental, spiritual, moral and social development." Child labor therefore is work, which involves a degree of exploitation, i.e., physical, mental and economic. It denies joy to children and denies access to social opportunities (like education, family love and attention), which eventually impairs personality and creativity, the evolution and growth of full being, and the health and mental development of a child. The problem of child labor therefore does not constitute the age or work of a child, but its exploitation and abuse. The perception of what constitutes exploitation or abuse can be subjective, as it is not easy to differentiate between the socialization aspects of a child's activity and its exploitative aspects.

Numbers and Distribution

Estimates vary but one often cited figure is that the number of children living independently in the streets totals between 100 million and 150 million worldwide. Estimating numbers of 'street children' is fraught with difficulties. In 1989, UNICEF estimated 100 million children were growing up on urban streets around the world. 14 years later UNICEF reported: "The latest estimates put the numbers of these children as high as 100 million" (UNICEF, 2002: 37). And even more recently: "The exact number of street children is impossible to quantify, but the figure almost certainly runs into tens of millions across the world. It is likely that the numbers are increasing" (UNICEF, 2005: 40-41). The 100 million figures are still commonly cited, but have no basis. In fact it is debatable whether the number of street children is growing globally or whether it is society's new found awareness of the reality of street children which has grown.

Distribution

While there are understandable pressures for policies to be informed by aggregate numbers, estimates of street child populations, even at city levels, are often hotly disputed and can distract rather than inform policy makers. Street children may be found on every inhabited continent in a large majority of the world's cities. The following estimates indicate the global extent of street child populations.

Statistics: UNICEF, 2005[30]

History

A child making his home/livelihood on the street is not a new or modern phenomenon. Orphaned and abandoned children have been a source of misery from earliest times. In fact, "Concerning abandoned children: there is general complaint that they are nowadays exposed more to dogs than to kindness."[24] In Tsarist Russia, seventeenth-century sources described destitute youths roaming the streets, and the phenomenon survived every attempt at eradication thereafter. In 1848 Lord Ashley referred to more than 30,000 'naked, filthy, roaming lawless and deserted children', in and around London. By 1922 there were at least 7 million homeless children in Russia as a result of nearly a decade of devastation from World War I and the Russian Civil War. Abandoned children formed gangs, created their own argot, and engaged in petty theft and prostitution.

Causes

As said previously children may end up on the streets for several basic reasons. Many children also work in the streets because their earnings are needed by their families. But, homes and families are part of the larger society and the underlying reasons for the poverty or breakdown of homes and families may be social, economic, political or environmental or any combination of these.

In a 1993 report, WHO offered the following list of causes for the growing problem of street children:[25]

- family breakdown
- armed conflict
- poverty
- natural and man-made disasters
- famine
- physical and sexual abuse
- exploitation by adults
- dislocation through migration
- urbanization and overcrowding
- acculturation
- disinheritance or being disowned

The orphaning of children as a result of HIV/AIDS is another cause that might be added to this list. More kids flee because of abuse than poverty. In India, contrary to popular myth, more children leave home due to a disturbed domestic environment than abject poverty, according to a report from the Ahmadabad Study Action Group (ASAG) and the Gujarat Institute of Development Research (GIDR). The study ranks familial harassment as the top reason behind children running away from home.[26]

Country wide statistics of the street kids

Russia

In Russia, street children usually find a home in underground pipe and cable collectors during the harsh winter. These underground homes offer space, shelter and most importantly of all, heat from hot water and central heating pipes. Russia has 1 million street children, and one in four crimes involves underage youths. Officially, the number of children without supervision is more than 700,000. However, experts believe the real figure has long been between 2 and 4 million.

India

India has the largest population of street children in the world. At least 18 million children live or work on the streets of urban India. The majority of these children are involved in crime, prostitution, gang related violence and drug trafficking. Conservative estimates state that about 300,000 children in India are engaged in commercial sex.[27] The Republic of India is the seventh largest and second most populous country in the world. With acceleration in economic growth, India has become one of the fastest growing developing countries. This has created a rift between the poor and the rich; 22 percent of the population lives below the income poverty line. Owing to unemployment, increasing rural-urban migration, attraction of city life and a lack of political will, "the [International Labor Organization] ILO estimated that India has earned the dubious distinction of having the largest child labour force in the world."[28] Although the government of India has taken some corrective measures and declared child labor illegal,[29] street children are subject to a variety of ills and abuse, including: malnutrition, hunger, health problems, substance abuse, theft, sexual exploitation, harassment by city police and railway authorities, and physical and sexual abuse.

Vietnam

According to data by the Street Educators' Club, the number of street children in Vietnam has shrunk from 21,000 in 2003 to 8,000 in 2007. The number dropped from 1,507 to 113 in Hanoi and from 8,507 to 794 in Ho Chi Minh City. In the meantime, the number of migrant children is increasing. This number is, however, unconfirmed owing to varying definitions of street children. Some experts mention several different categories of street children in Vietnam: "children who have run away from home or who have no home, and who sleep on the street; children who sleep on the street with their family or guardian; children who have a family or guardian and who usually sleep at home, but work on the streets; economic migrants who rent rooms with other working children; and bonded laborers".[30]

There are almost 400 humanitarian organizations and international non-governmental organizations providing help for about 15,000 children who live in especially difficult conditions.

Classification of Street Children

UNICEF defines "Street children are those for whom the street (in the widest sense of the word, i.e., unoccupied dwellings, wastelands, etc.) more than their family has become their real home, a situation in which there is no protection, supervision or direction from responsible adults. These street children live on footpaths, parks or on the street itself. Some of them may spend their full time on the streets and others may spend part of their time to generate their income.[31] They are classified into three categories.

Children on the street are those engaged in begging, selling items and engaging in menial jobs to support the family. They are in touch with their families and some of them even go home by evening to contribute their earnings. Some of "these children have nothing to do in their homes so they frequently roam the streets, returning home only at night or at meal time."[32] In the course of time, these children get addicted to habits that exclude them from their homes.

Children of the street actually live on the street or outside of a normal family environment. Family ties may exist but they are discarded from the families due to various reasons. Even though they have families at home they live a lonely life on the streets and struggle for survival. They may have occasional family contact.

Children in the streets with no family contact at all consider the streets as their full time home. They actually live in the streets without family ties. They depend on the streets for food, shelter and survival. This kind of group easily gets attracted towards drugs and other underground activities that lead them to a life of crime. Nandna Reddy identifies these children as "roofless and rootless" who live and work on the streets.[33]

Even though there are different definitions and classifications of street children, this study considers the third classification, 'Children in the streets'. Since there are several categories of street children, the focus of this paper is restricted to children who run away from home.

Classification of Working Children

Working children can also be classified as:

Domestic Working Children

This includes children who undertake duties for domestic purposes like caring for younger siblings, cooking, cleaning, washing, fetching water, etc. These tasks are mostly performed by girls. Although domestic service need not be hazardous, children in domestic servitude may well be the most vulnerable and exploited children, as they are most difficult to protect, due to the hidden nature of the work. These children remain away from basic elementary education.

Non-domestic and Non-monetary Work

This is a major form of child activity in subsistence economies, and encompasses farming, hunting, gathering and household/cottage industrial activities. In an agrarian economy like India, children spend a great deal of time in such activities as looking after the cattle, grazing goats, collecting fodder and scaring away birds. They become gradually involved in full-time agricultural work. Naturally such children are deprived of schooling, play and social activity, which impede their mental development and creativity. Children under this category, whether in agriculture, plantation or in cottage industry are engaged either independently or as part of family labor.

Chapter 3

Problems, Implications and Response

The Problem of Street Children

They flock to the town hoping to have a better life. Once there, they easily pick up small jobs and their initial earnings make them complacent. With a little money in their pocket for a meal, a pack of cigarettes and a movie, they feel like adults, but not for long. Soon, they fall prey to unscrupulous middlemen and gangs and are often caught up in a life of crime and violence. Some of them are deliberately maimed and mutilated.

On the Streets where they live

Delhi's street children have set up an alternative forum for themselves. They meet, discuss problems, and even publish their own newspaper. There are 400,000 street children in Delhi. The capital's streets and roads are their workplace. For 100,000 of these children, the streets double as home. They have nowhere else to go. Street children work as rag-pickers, in tea-stalls and dhabhas (roadside eateries), as shoeshine boys or vendors. But, street life can be unpleasant and risky. They face physical abuse, the callousness of policemen, and are vulnerable to drugs and to adverse health conditions.[34]

Police Abuse

Indian street children are routinely detained illegally, beaten and tortured and sometimes killed by police. Several factors contribute to this phenomenon: police perceptions of street children, widespread corruption and a culture of police violence, the inadequacy and non-implementation of legal safeguards, and the level of impunity that law enforcement officials enjoy. Harassment, threats, insults, exploitation and physical and sexual abuse may be carried out directly by the police, or by other members of the public with either the active or tacit encouragement of the police. The police are therefore doubly responsible for human rights' violations - as perpetrators themselves, and for failing to protect children from abuse by others. The police may also be guilty of using their power to extort sexual favors, money, or free child labor from street children.

Sexual Abuse

Many of the street children who have run away from home have done so because they were beaten or sexually abused. In fact they face sexual harassment from adults and their peer group. Girls are easily exploited and are gradually introduced to prostitution. Sexually abused children are prone to sexually transmitted diseases such as HIV / AIDS. Tragically, their homelessness can lead to further abuse through exploitative child labor and prostitution. Not only does abuse rob runaway children of their material security, it also leaves them emotionally scarred. Many of the abused children are traumatized and some refuse to speak for months. To aggravate matters, children often feel guilty and blame themselves for their mistreatment. Such damage can take years to recover from in even the most loving of environments; on the streets it may never heal. In damning statistics, a government study has found that a vast majority of street children face sexual abuse in India, which is home to the world's largest number of destitute children. According to a study conducted by the Ministry of Women and Child Development, the overall incidence of physical abuse among street children was 66.8

per cent. The majority of the street children facing physical abuse are in the age group of 5-12 years. Around 55 per cent of the street children reported having undergone sexual abuse.[35]

Drug Addiction

Street children often become addicted to various substances and drugs. They live and work amidst trash, animals and open sewers. Not only are they exposed and susceptible to disease, they are also unlikely to be vaccinated or to receive medical treatment. Only two in three Indian children have been vaccinated against TB, Diphtheria, Tetanus, Polio and Measles; only one in ten against Hepatitis B. Most street children have not been vaccinated at all. They usually cannot afford, and do not trust, doctors or medicines. If they receive any treatment at all it will often be harmful, as with children whose parents misguidedly place scalding metal on their bellies as a remedy for persistent stomach pain. Child laborers suffer from exhaustion, injury, exposure to dangerous chemicals, plus muscle and bone afflictions.

Child Labor

Most Indian street children work. In Jaipur, a common job is rag-picking, in which boys and girls as young as 6 years old sift through garbage in order to collect recyclable material. The children usually rise before dawn and carry their heavy load in a large bag over their shoulder. Rag-pickers can be seen alongside pigs and dogs searching through trash heaps on their hands and knees. Other common jobs are collecting firewood, tending to animals, street vending, dyeing cloth, begging, prostitution and domestic labor. Children who work are not only subject to the strains and hazards of their labor, they are also denied the education or training that could enable them to escape the poverty trap.

Health

Poor health is a chronic problem for street children. Half of all children in India are malnourished, but for street children the proportion is much higher. These children are not only underweight, but their growth has often been stunted; for example, it is very common to mistake a 12 year old for an 8 year old.

Living on the streets can cause many major health problems. Some of these may include physical, sexual, and mental health problems that are difficult to relieve. Because of a lack of proper medical care, street children are more inclined to experience physical health problems such as diseases from contaminated water and air. "Several studies have confirmed that around 80% of street children use drugs regularly."[36] At a young age they start to consume drugs which ultimately can retard physical growth. Also children are more sexually active while living on the streets and can be exposed to many diseases through this activity. "An outreach program in Honduras reported that 85% of sexually active street children had been treated for a sexually transmitted disease."[37] To obtain money, food, clothing, and shelter they may engage in "survival sex" with adults. This lifestyle, which is basically prostitution, causes not only sexually transmitted diseases but also teen pregnancy. Customers harass these victims by saying, "I won't buy any of your chewing gum, but will buy you."[38] Many of the young girls who are victims of prostitution have no sense of pride or the indignity of their situation; they simply have no control of their destiny. Mental problems include underdeveloped motor skills, illiteracy, and others. These children do not obtain or learn the simple developmental skills that help them find their own identity.

Homelessness

Street children in India may be homeless because their family is homeless through poverty or migration, or because they have been abandoned, orphaned or have run away. It is not unusual to see whole families living on the sidewalks of Jaipur, or rows of individual children sleeping around the railway station.

Homeless children have the odds stacked against them. They are exposed to the elements, have an uncertain supply of food, are likely to miss out on education and medical treatment, and are at a high risk of suffering addiction, abuse and illness. A single child alone on the streets is especially vulnerable.

Poverty

Poverty is the primary cause of the street children crisis. Poverty dumps a crowd of problems onto a child. Not only do these problems cause immediate suffering, they also conspire to keep the child poor throughout his/her life. In order to survive, a poor child in India may well be forced to sacrifice education and training; without skills the child will grow into an adult who remains at the bottom of the economic heap.

Crimes and Violence

Street Children face many hardships while living on the streets, away from support systems and family. As part of this life of violence and marginality, the majority of street children have been arrested at least once, use drugs, and engage in illegal activities. They work, beg and steal to survive, but for most of them getting a job would be an improvement to their life, as they consider street life as the 'bad path.' The police perceive these children to be dangerous and criminals because of the lifestyle that many of these children are forced to adopt. Bad habits form because no structured way of living persists among these children. They start to form these habits by first running errands for their seniors and soon many of these anti-social activities become a way of life for them and they begin to doing them for themselves. They start using tobacco, alcohol, and indulge in gambling. Because they do not have any role models or guidance, they think that these activities are the norm. "It's easier to get through the day when my head is full of crack," says Lucio, a fifteen year old boy who has been living on the streets for several years. "I get less scared, you know; I can sleep well. And I don't give a damn about anything. I see a watch that I want and I just snatch it and split"[39]. For these children it is easy to obtain drugs such as crack and cocaine, drugs which allows them to not worry about the hardships they face on a day to day basis. The police are supposed to protect each street child. Each child has an individual right to be treated like a child. Police officers have been accused and taken to trial many times for acts of violence perpetrated against street children.

Bonded Child Labor

Tied or bonded labor is a manifestation of a "feudal or semi-feudal" structure of society and the economy. Children are bonded both in the agriculture sector and in the nonagricultural sector. The principal feature bonded labor is the pledging of children against a loan (small or large), or an agreement between a child's parents and an employer, whereby the child would work throughout or for part of his or her life in exchange for money or food. Their lifelong servitude never succeeds even in reducing the debt. Children are "lured away or pledged" by their parents for paltry sums of money. Most of them are kept in captivity, tortured and made to work 12 to 16 hours a day."[40] The reasons for bondage could be the immediate need for money (for purposes like medical treatment, repayment of an earlier loan, marriage of daughters, etc.) or an agreement to replace the bonded worker with a healthier sibling child worker.

Wage Labor

Wage labor is one of the major types of work activity for children. Wage labor includes work in domestic service, cottage industries, manufacturing processes, industries, and other service activities. Wage laborers work either as a part of the family labor force or as wage workers. They are often preferred to adults, because they garner low wages, their docile nature and pliability. Wages are paid on a piece rate basis, applying tremendous pressure to work faster. Hours of work tend to be long.[41]

Commercial and Sexual Exploitation of Children

Commercial and sexual exploitation, especially for girls, is common worldwide. Girls are lured or forced into this form of hazardous labor, which can verge on slavery. The physical and psychological damage inflicted by commercial sexual exploitation makes it one of the most hazardous forms of child labor. These children are not only subjected to the risk of HIV/AIDS, sexually transmitted diseases, unwanted pregnancies and drug addiction, but are also plunged into a distorted reality where "violence and distrust, shame and rejection are the norms."[42]

The Child Combatant

This is another form of labor exploitation, very much discussed currently at the national and international level. This could be the most difficult challenge in the new millennium. There is a need to address the pull and push factors, which facilitate the recruitment of children as soldiers. These factors range from education to gainful employment. There is a certain amount of prestige that comes from "being a hero." Even though we rehabilitate child combatants who have surrendered to government forces, when they return to their community they rejoin as combatants if they fail to secure the promised employment. We have to identify the most appropriate strategies to sustain their withdrawal and to prevent others from joining as combatants. We have to focus on the training of war trauma counselors to address the psychological impact created in the minds of war combatants. Shelters and other supporting facilities should be in place to accommodate the victims.

Gender Discrimination

In Indian society females are often discriminated against. Their health, education, prosperity and freedom are all impacted. The problem is worse in conservative Rajasthan than almost anywhere else in India. Because girls carry the liability of dowry and leave the family home after marriage, parents may prefer to have male offspring. Many female babies are aborted, abandoned or deliberately neglected and underfed simply because they are girls. This can be seen in the fact that the female mortality rate amongst 0-4 year olds in India is 106% of the male mortality rate, whereas the comparable number in Western Europe is 74%. The rate is 119% in Rajasthan. Further evidence of the imbalance is that the female/male ratio within the general population of India is unnaturally low at 927/1000 and even lower in Rajasthan at 909/1000.

Gender discrimination is particularly evident in the area of education, where boys are more likely to attend school and continue their education for a longer period of time. Traditionally, the place of the woman is regarded as being in the home and many parents and children consider education for girls to be a waste of time, an unnecessary distraction from work or domestic chores. The gender parity of adult literacy between men and women is 29%.

Child marriage is another way in which girls are disadvantaged. In addition to limiting educational possibilities and stunting personal development, early marriage carries health risks. A girl under 15 is five times more likely to die during pregnancy than a woman in her twenties; her child is also more likely to die.

Implications of Children Living on the Streets

Street children are susceptible to drug/alcohol addiction and to the use of inhalants, such as cobbler's glue, correction fluid, gold/silver spray paint, nail polish, rubber cement, permanent/dry erase markers and gasoline. These substances offer them an escape from reality, and take away the gnawing pangs of hunger. In exchange, they invite a host of physical and psychological problems, including hallucinations, pulmonary edema, kidney failure, and irreversible brain damage. Glue sniffing is a pragmatic response to an unlivable situation. Street children sniff glue because it "takes away" their hunger, cold, and despair. It also gives them the "courage" to steal and engage in survival sex. But, glue also causes irreparable damage and even death, and keeps children stuck in the streets. Once addicted their personalities change. They become more aggressive. Glue destroys any future dreams these children might have once envisaged for themselves. They become enslaved to the vapors.[43] In order to secure the regular dose of drugs/alcohol and inhalants they resort to pickpocketing, petty theft and, often, more serious crimes. Many of these children eventually turn into hardened criminals controlled by organized crime rings for drug trafficking, prostitution and other unlawful activities, thus placing a heavy burden on the law and order machinery. Street children are routinely detained illegally, beaten and tortured by their employers, the police and other members of the mainstream society who extract the maximum labor from them. Several factors contribute to this phenomenon, such as the inadequacy and non-implementation of legal safeguards, and the level of impunity that law enforcement officials enjoy. These street children are generally viewed as vagrants and criminals. While it is true that street children are sometimes involved in petty theft, drug trafficking, prostitution and other criminal activities, very few attempts are made to examine the root cause for such activities and provide soothing and caring comfort to rehabilitate them. Street children are also easy targets for police atrocities"[44]. The responses from the authorities are to remove children forcibly from the streets, often to incarcerate them, and sometimes to resort to violent measures. Gross abuse is often quietly sanctioned against them. There are reports of street children being beaten, tortured and even murdered by police. They are young, small, poor, and ignorant of their rights and often have no family members who will come to their defense. It does not require much time or effort to detain and beat a child in order to extract a confession, and the children are unlikely to register formal complaints.

Implication of Inappropriate Work for Children

Work has always been an important avenue of learning and socialization. Children have a powerful desire for competence, and this is expressed and satisfied through work as well as play. The work may be beneficial, providing or enhancing a child's physical, mental, spiritual, moral or social development. The productive use of children in the family work could provide the process of learning, the skills for a particular trade or craft. This could help the child to turn into a reasonably proficient craftsman or a skilled worker. Thus childhood work, paid or unpaid, might become an investment for at least a modest future. Nearly all the child workers in this category live with their families. This category of child worker, where there is no interference with schooling (formal or non-formal), recreation, and rest, cannot be viewed as exploitative. But, at the same time the work by children, purely for profit, cannot be justified at the cost of the child's health, education and mental, physical and psychological development. The work takes a heavy toll physically, emotionally and intellectually. They are subjected to all kinds of occupational hazards and diseases, as they are frequently more vulnerable because of their growing bodies, their lower threshold for toxins and their lesser ability to respond effectively to hazards. Children are especially vulnerable to accidents because they have neither the awareness of the dangers nor knowledge of the precautions to be taken at work. It is often found that children and young workers tend to have more serious accidents than adults. The presence of children in these occupations will affect their life and limbs, their health, their psyche and their total development. Children working long hours suffer from excessive fatigue and are susceptible to infectious diseases. Stunted growth is common among the working children. The work performed is frequently too demanding in relation to their size and strength, causing irreversible damage to their physical and physiological development, resulting in permanent disabilities, with serious consequences for their adult lives. In some occupations, children are exposed for long hours every day to toxic fumes or industrial waste. Children are particularly sensitive to exposure to solvents, lead, mercury and benzene. These toxic substances are handled by children in leather, construction activity, glass works, repair of automobiles, and mining activities. The effects of repetitive action, and postures of sitting, like in the case of carpet weaving, can result in muscular-skeletal damage permanently. Carrying heavy loads or being forced to adopt unnatural positions at work can permanently distort or disable growing bodies. Some work situations expose children to unprotected machinery, the risk of explosions and industrial accidents such as in the case of fireworks, glasswork, etc. The work may damage their eyesight. A less visible form of exploitation against children is commercial sexual exploitation. It is one of the most brutal forms of violence against children. The child victims suffer extreme physical, psychosocial and emotional abuse, which have life-long adverse consequences. They risk early pregnancy, maternal mortality, sexually transmitted diseases and HIV/AIDS. Sexual exploitation of children has significant emotional ramifications as the victims are unable to return to a normal way of life and are psychologically scarred by the experience. In Mumbai, India many young prostitutes were found to have sexually transmitted diseases with a significant proportion of cases having AIDS.[45] The girls are often the victims of beatings, verbal abuse and sexual molestation and rape in the brothels. The inappropriate work and living conditions in the city streets harms them indirectly by depriving them of positive experiences for a future life. They remain bereft of education, play and rest, the basic requirements for mental, physical and psychological development. The opportunities lost for learning and growth reduce their chances of prosperity in life and contribute to the perpetuation of increasing poverty and social underdevelopment from generation to generation.

Government and Non-Government Responses

Government Initiatives for Street Children

Because they have not reached the age of majority, street children have no representation in the governing process. They have no vote themselves nor by proxy through their parents, from whom they likely are alienated. Nor do street children have any economic leverage. Consequently, governments may pay little attention to them. The rights of street children are often ignored by governments even though nearly all of the world's governments have ratified the U.N. Convention on the Rights of the Child.[46]

Governments are often embarrassed by street children and may blame parents or neighboring countries. Non-Governmental Organizations (NGOs) may also be blamed for encouraging children to live in the streets by making street life more bearable or attractive through the services they provide.

When governments implement programs to deal with street children, these generally involve placing the children in orphanages, juvenile homes or correctional institutes. However, some children are in the streets because they have fled from such institutions and some governments prefer to support or work in partnership with NGO programs. Governments sometimes institute roundups when they remove all the children from city streets and either forcibly relocate them elsewhere or incarcerate them. In the most extreme cases, governments may tacitly accept or participate in social cleansing operations that murder street children.

The Ministry of Social Justice and Empowerment has prepared an integrated program for street children. The increase in the number of street children, orphans, destitute, neglected and delinquent children is a matter of great concern to the Ministry of Social Justice and Empowerment. Recognizing the basic responsibility of the government towards these children, specific schemes are being put into effect, to provide immediate relief and succor to these children as well as to meet their long-term developmental needs. The basic objective of the program is to provide for wholesome development of children without homes and family ties and prevent destitution. The essential components of the program include provision of shelter, nutrition, health care, sanitation and hygiene, safe drinking water, education, recreational facilities and protection against abuse and exploitation to destitute and neglected street children.

All the states' capitals and cities with a population of 1 million or more are covered under this program. The scheme is already operational in 23 cities across the country. Under the program, grants-in-aid are provided to NGOs and other Voluntary Organizations and there were an estimated 32,451 beneficiaries under the ongoing projects of the program between 1991-2000. Up to 90 per cent financial assistance is being provided to NGOs as well as to other local bodies for a wide range of program initiatives that include:[47]

- ⇨ Contact program offering counseling, guidance and referral services to destitute and neglected children;
- ⇨ Establishment of 24-hour drop-in-shelters for street children with facilities for night stay, safe drinking water, bathing, latrines, first aid and recreation;
- ⇨ Education for Street and Working Children in India on-formal education programs imparting literacy, numeracy and life education;
- ⇨ Programs for the reintegration of children with their families;
- ⇨ Programs for the enrolment of children in schools including full support for subsistence, education, nutrition, recreation, etc.;
- ⇨ Programs providing facilities for training in meaningful vocations; Programs for occupational placement;
- ⇨ Programs aimed at mobilizing preventive health services and providing access to treatment facilities;
- ⇨ Programs aimed at reducing the incidence of drug and substance abuse, HIV/AIDS and STDs and other chronic health disorders amongst street children;
- ⇨ Program aimed at providing recreational facilities;

- ⇨ Programs for capacity building of NGOs, local bodies and state governments to undertake related responsibilities;
- ⇨ Programs for advocacy and awareness-building on child rights.

Under these programs, 69.504 million rupees were granted to 103 NGOs to support 32, 451 children in 37 cities throughout the country.[48] The aim was to provide both non-institutional and institutional services to the street children. The Ministry plans to simultaneously strengthen institutional services for the identified children. In particular, an effort is being made to check the deteriorating condition of children's homes, which have in the recent past been attracting adverse attention from the Parliament, the Courts, the National Human Rights Commission and the Media.

Child Help Line is a 24-hour free phone service, which can be accessed by dialing 1098. Child Line provides emergency assistance to children in distress and subsequently, based upon the child's need, the child is referred to an appropriate organization for long-term follow-up and care. The service focuses upon the needs of children living alone on the streets. This service is currently available at Mumbai, Delhi, Kolkata, Hyderabad, Nagpur, Varanasi, Chennai, Patna and Bangalore. The Child Line is operated in each city by a network of NGOs and the plan is to extend the service in the next two years to as many as 40 cities.

CHILDLINE is a platform bringing together the Ministry for Women & Child Development, Government of India, Department of Telecommunications, street and community youth, non-profit organizations, academic institutions, the corporate sector and concerned individuals.

CHILDLINE works for the protection of the rights of children in general, with a special focus on children in need of care and protection, especially the more vulnerable sections, which include:

- Street children and youth living alone on the streets
- Child laborers working in the unorganized and organized sectors
- Domestic help, especially girl domestics

- Children affected by physical / sexual / emotional abuse in family, schools or institutions.
- Children who need emotional support and guidance
- Children of commercial sex workers
- Child victims of the flesh trade
- Victims of child trafficking
- Children abandoned by parents or guardians
- Missing children
- Runaway children
- Children who are victims of substance abuse
- Differently-abled children
- Children in conflict with the law
- Children in institutions
- Mentally challenged children
- HIV/ AIDS infected children
- Children affected by conflict and disaster
- Child political refugees
- Children whose families are in crises

In 1996, Mumbai launched CHILDLINE, the country's first toll-free tele-helpline for street children in distress. It has responded a total of 15,883,547 calls from inception till March 2009 and operates in 83 cities/districts in 22 States and 3 Union Territories, through its network of 196 partner organizations across India.[49]

Government Initiatives for Working Children

The Government of India is greatly concerned about the magnitude and plight of the working children. India has stood for constitutional, statutory and development measures that are required to eliminate child labor. Six IL0 Conventions related to child labor have been ratified. The framers of the Indian Constitution consciously incorporated relevant provisions in the Constitution to secure labor protection for children (Articles 24 and 39 (e) and (f)) and compulsory universal elementary education (Article 45). However, the basic goal of compulsory education up to the age of 14 years has yet to be achieved owing to a lack of political commitment and will. Poor educational infrastructure in the villages is the major hurdle in the eradication of child labor. On the other hand, several laws have been passed periodically to prohibit or improve the working conditions of child labor. The legislation has started bearing fruit, but the situation demands strict enforcement along with creating conducive conditions for compulsory education. The government, realizing that mere legislation would be insufficient, adopted the National Policy for Children (NPC) in August 1974. The policy stated, "It shall be the policy of the state to provide adequate service to children both before and after birth and through the period of their growth, to ensure their full physical, mental and social development".[50]

The Child Labor (Prohibition and Regulation) Act (CLA), 1986, was enacted with a view to rationalizing earlier legislation on child labor, ensuring elimination of child labor in hazardous employment, and regulating the conditions of child labor in non-hazardous industries. One major loophole of the Act is that it only covers children in the organized sector and not the 90 per cent working in the unorganized sector. Moreover many occupations, which are hazardous, are not included in the Act. The government initiated several action-oriented programs to withdraw children from hazardous work and prevent them entering the labor markets again. The most significant step in this direction was the adoption of the National Policy of Education (NPE-1986) and National Policy on child labor (1987). The policy was formulated in conjunction with legal measures to address the social-economic issues having a bearing on child labor and to provide a framework for a concrete program of action. The policy encompasses action in the fields of education, health, nutrition, integrated child development and employment. Both these policies aimed at successfully rehabilitating children who were now, free from hazardous employment and reducing the incidence of child labor progressively. The opening of special schools for imparting Non-formal Education Programme (NFE) and vocational training was the major recommendation of the two policies.

The National Child Labor Policy (NCLP) approved in 1987 envisaged a project based Plan of Action to reduce the incidence of child labor in the hazardous occupations. The basic objective was to rehabilitate the children withdrawn from hazardous employments. The policy consisted of three main programs:

- Legal Action Plan: To effectively enforce legal provisions related to child labor under various laws of the country.
- Focusing on general development programs: To effectively utilize the ongoing development programs of different departments/ministries for the benefit of the target families. Hence, convergence of actions from several departments was required.
- Project-Based Plan of Action: To establish special schools for the rehabilitation of children withdrawn from hazardous occupations in the areas of high concentration of child labor. Ten areas with high incidence of child labor in hazardous industries were initially identified.[57]

The Industries identified were:

- ⇨ The match industry in Sivakasi, Tamil Nadu
- ⇨ The diamond polishing industry in Surat, Gujarat
- ⇨ The precious stone polishing industry in Jaipur (Rajasthan)
- ⇨ The glass industry in Firozabad (Uttar Pradesh)
- ⇨ The brassware industry in Moradabad (Uttar Pradesh)
- ⇨ The handmade carpet industry in Mirzapur-Bhadohi (Uttar Pradesh)
- ⇨ The lock-making industry in Aligarh (Uttar Pradesh)
- ⇨ The handmade carpet Industry in Jammu and Kashmir
- ⇨ The slate industry in Mandsaur (Madhya Pradesh)

A Project Society has been established in the National Child Labor Project areas for an Integration of various developmental programs. The job of the Project Society is to:

- Effectively enforce child labor laws.
- Identify of areas for starting Non-Formal Education through the opening of the special schools.
- Create public awareness, through adult education, income generation and the creation of employment opportunities for target families.

Target children (children working in hazardous occupations, who have not reached 14 years of age) are to be enrolled in the special schools. The scheme envisaged non-formal education, vocational training, supplementary nutrition, regular health care and stipends in case the children were withdrawn from prohibited employments and vocations. It also envisaged the extension of benefits of the other State Government programs for these school children and their families by the district administration as far as possible. The desired teaching mode should preferably be non-formal with a condensed syllabus for a maximum period of 3 years. After the completion of the 3 years of special school education, children are expected to join the formal stream of education in the 6th standard. While appreciating the need for flexibility in the curriculum, the scheme felt the need to introduce some uniformity in the syllabus.

The curriculum, course content and textual material needed was desired to be finalized at the state/district level by associating State Council Educational Research and Training (SCERT), District Institute for Education and Training (DIET), UNICEF and other NGOs with experience in this field. The program also stipulated imparting age-appropriate craft and pre-vocational training, keeping in view the resources and market forces of the area, so that children unable to join formal schools after 14 years of age could start their own occupations. The government of India is implementing NCLP in 93 districts of the country as on June 2000.

There are two types of special schools, one with an approved strength of 50 children and the other with 100 children. Each of the project societies has been authorized to run a specified number of schools. These schools are managed by the project society or alternatively the project society runs these schools through local NGOs. About 1,55,250 children were covered in 2,571 schools under the NCLP scheme. (Table No. IV.2) in a landmark judgment, issued on 10 December 1996. In writ petition (Civil) No. 465/1986, the Supreme Court of India gave the same directions, regarding the manner in which children working in hazardous occupations as defined in (CLA, 86) are to be withdrawn from work and to be simultaneously rehabilitated. The direction was also given to regulate and improve working conditions in non-hazardous occupations.

Several measures were proposed by the Supreme Court to solve the problem of child labor.

The measures include:

- ⇨ Conducting a survey to identify working children.
- ⇨ Withdrawing children from hazardous industries and ensuring their education in appropriate institutions.
- ⇨ Contributing of Rs. 20,000 per child to be paid by the offending employers of children to a welfare fund to be established for this purpose.
- ⇨ Employing at least one adult member of the family of a child removed from hazardous work, and if that is not possible, making a contribution of Rs. 5,000 per child to the welfare fund of the state government.
- ⇨ Providing financial assistance to the families of the children so withdrawn to be paid out of the interest earnings on the surplus of Rs. 20,000/25,000 deposited in the welfare fund as long as the child is actually sent to school.

Regulating hours of work for children working in non-hazardous occupations, so that their working hours do not exceed six hours per day and education for at least two hours is ensured. Requiring the employer to bear the entire cost of the education of the children employed.

International and Voluntary Sector Initiatives

Non-government organizations employ a wide variety of strategies to address the needs and rights of street children. These may be categorized as follows:

- Advocacy - through media and government contacts, agencies may press for the rights of street children to be respected.
- Preventive - programs that work to prevent children from taking to the streets, through family and community support and education.
- Residential rehabilitation programs - some agencies provide an environment isolated from the streets where

activities are focused on assisting children to recover from drug, physical or sexual abuse.

- Full-care residential homes - the final stage in many agencies' programs is when the child is no longer in the streets but lives completely in an environment provided by the agency. Some agencies promote fostering children to individual families. Others set up group homes where a small number of children live together with house parents employed by the agency. Others set up institutional care centers catering to large numbers of children. Some agencies include a follow-up program that monitors and counsels children and families after the child has left the residential program.
- Street-based programs - these work to alleviate the worst aspects of street life for children by providing services to them in the streets. These programs tend to be less expensive and serve a larger number of street children than institutional programs since the children still must provide for themselves in the streets.

⇨ feeding program
⇨ medical services
⇨ legal assistance
⇨ street education
⇨ financial services (banking and entrepreneur programs)
⇨ family reunification
⇨ drop-in centers/night shelters
⇨ outreach programs designed to bring the children into closer contact with the agency

- Conscience-raising - changing the attitude of the street children to their circumstances and enabling them to view themselves as an oppressed minority and to become protagonists rather than passive recipients of aid.

Many agencies employ several of these strategies and a child will pass through a number of stages before he or she "graduates". First he/she will be contacted by an outreach program, and then may become involved in drop-in center programs, though still living in the streets. Later, the child may be accepted into a halfway house and finally into residential care where he or she becomes fully divorced from street life.[51]

Monetary and technical support has been provided to the government and NGOs for various welfare programs for the children in difficult circumstances by U.N. agencies and other international and national donor agencies. The support from U.N. agencies has come from ILO, UNESCO, UNICEF, UNIFEM, UNFPA, UNDP, and the World Bank. In addition to these, foreign governmental agencies like USAID, DFID, and the Norwegian and German governments have also supported specific programs in the specific areas.

International Labor Organization (ILO)

Two parallel programs intended to build financial and human capacity of the government and non-government agencies were started in India with the support from ILO.

i) International Programme on the Elimination of Child Labour (IPEC).
ii) Child Labor Action Support Programme (CLASP)

IPEC, is a global initiative of the ILO. It was launched in 1992 to support participating member countries in their national efforts to combat and eliminate child labor progressively based on ILO Conventions, in particular, Convention No. 138. The programs have been implemented through Various Action programs, selected by the National Steering Committee of the Ministry of Labor. The Action Program was characterized by:

- ⇨ Setting up non-formal education centers for working children in these identified areas.
- ⇨ Supplementing nutritional and health care.
- ⇨ Carry out awareness-raising project for the children, their parents and community, and employers.
- ⇨ Eliciting community support and involvement for sustainability and continuation of welfare programs.

- ⇨ Training programs for labor inspectors for effective enforcement of child labor legislation.

Under the ILO-IPEC program, a sum of US $6.9 million or 270 million rupees was made available to central employees' organizations, central trade union organizations and NGOs between 1992-1999.[52]

This amount has been utilized by160 projects benefiting about 100,000 children.[53] The scheme was extended until December 21, 2001 and was extendable for a further period of one year. The government of Germany aided the CLASP program. Assistance taken under this program has been used for the purpose of supporting ongoing activities under the National Policy on Child Labor.

United Nations International Children's Educational Fund (UNICEF)

UNICEF acknowledges the need to advocate for the implementation of the Convention on the Rights of the Child in India and promote mandatory education. A number of international seminars, symposia, workshops and conferences were organized or supported by UNICEF highlighting the problems of illiteracy among children. UNICEF in India initiated curriculum programs and a supply of books for children. It funded studies on the situational analysis of street children in the major cities of India. Currently UNICEF is supporting the Bal Adhikar Pariyojana Programme providing needs-based education to out-of-school children in the carpet-weaving belt of Mirzapur and Bhadhoi. The aims and objectives of UNICEF programs are to:

- ⇨ Advocate for the revision and enforcement of legislation to prohibit child labor, particularly in hazardous industries;
- ⇨ Assist central and state governments with an action plan for the withdrawal and rehabilitation of child labor.
- ⇨ Strengthen the alliance between NGOs, media and industry for social mobilization in support of the elimination of child labor.

United Nations Educational, Scientific and Cultural Organization (UNESCO)

UNESCO has been actively working for street children and working children in India since the 1990 World Conference on Education for All, held in Jomtien, and the World Declaration on Education for All. The UNESCO's Education Programme for Children in need has enabled the organization to provide substantial funding and technical support for educational activities in favor of children in difficult circumstances. At the World Education Forum held in Dakar in April 2000 UNESCO was given the mandate of a lead agency to promote and implement the Education for All movement. It was supported by other official partners in this regard, such as the World Bank, UNFPA, UNDP and UNICEF. UNESCO is to play a key role in helping to co-ordinate policy planning at a national, regional and international level to ensure that all children have access to free and compulsory primary education of good quality by 2015. Special emphasis is to be given to girls and children from ethnic minorities who were facing difficult circumstances. The framework is also directed at eliminating gender disparities in primary and secondary education by 2005 and achieving gender equality in education by 2015. At the national level, concrete plans providing technical assistance and aid for achieving Education for All will be augmented for those countries that do not have co-ordination mechanisms. UNESCO aims to collaborate with government and other agencies at the local level in encouraging the mobilization of the necessary resources; the establishment of sector analysis and project design; and their implementation with the aid of experts. UNESCO is also devoted to holding regional and sub-regional technical meetings enabling all the bilateral and multilateral partners, like the regional development banks, representatives of the Ministries of Education and Finance, teachers' unions, the private sector, civil society foundations and parents to discuss the regions' needs in terms of basic education and modalities of co-operation and financing within the framework of Education For All.

UNESCO has been supporting CINI ASHA and Don Bosco Ashaiayam, NGOs based in Calcutta since 1997 with regard to a framework of programs providing for the survival, growth and development of street and working children. This active support from

UNESCO has contributed significantly in providing rehabilitation and education for street and working children in Kolkata's urban agglomeration. UNESCO is also supporting PRAYAS, a Delhi-based NGO in preparing a project to develop innovative educational material to accomplish the needs of street and working children for education in urban surroundings. The educational material prepared will be tested for application by other NGOs in the country. UNESCO has also supported the present study in the context of assessing the magnitude of out-of-school children in difficult circumstances, and to evaluate the present implementation of education and other rehabilitation programs, undertaken by the government and NGOs for these children. The aim is to prepare a coordinated strategy for achieving the Dakar Declaration of Education for All by 2015. UNESCO organized a workshop on 15 December 2000 to discuss the results of the study and to come up with a concerted strategy after thorough discussions with the representatives from government, NGOs, UN agencies, International Aid agencies, and other civil societies.

Other Agencies

The other U.N. agencies such as the UNDP and the World Bank are supporting educational projects in the Mirzapur-Bhadhoi carpet weaving belt for out-of-school children. International government agencies such as USAID, DFID, and the German and Norwegian governments are also supporting several NGOs with education and rehabilitation schemes in several cities of the country. Other international donor agencies supporting child education and rehabilitation programs are:

- ⇨ Terra Des Hommes, Bread for the World, Rugmark Foundation, Care and Fair, Misesior (Germany)
- ⇨ Christian Aid, Anti Slavery-International, and Project Mala (United Kingdom)
- ⇨ Asian American Free Labor Institute, Child Labor Coalition and International Labor Rights Education and Research Fund, National Consumer League (United States)

- ⇨ Radda Barmer BLLF (Sweden)
- ⇨ Save the Children (United Kingdom and Canada)
- ⇨ Alternative for India Development (United Kingdom)
- ⇨ Child Relief and You
- ⇨ S.O.S. Schools

In addition, several national voluntary organizations are supporting the initiatives of NGOs through human resources, technical, and monetary help. The South Asian Coalition on Child Servitude (SACCS), a conglomerate of NGOs working for children was actively associated with the Global March against Child Labor which took place to create awareness of child labor. Several children were released from the bondage of hazardous labor by the organization.

Chapter 4

Street Children in Vijayawada and Rehabilitation Work

Street Children in Vijayawada

A 1989 report by UNICEF estimated the number of street children in Vijayawada to be 19,800. This figure includes those who live in the streets or in railway stations; those who are orphans and homeless; and those from the surrounding slums who work/roam in the streets. The Forum for Child Rights estimates that on average 33 children arrives at the Vijayawada railway station every day. The typical street child is a male, between 11 and 13 years of age; a majority of them hail from other towns and villages within Andhra Pradesh; most are Hindu and belong to castes that the government designated as "backward."[54] There are about 19,000 street children and working children in Vijayawada.[55]

Seasonal Dimension of the Issue

Though the influx of street children is perennial in nature, it does vary from season to season. Mostly the children arrive at the end of the agricultural seasons and when the academic examination results are announced. Each and every year, the first wave of street children arrives when the agricultural operation comes to a grinding halt. At that time landless laborers become redundant and unemployed, leading to the vicious cycle of scarcity, deprivation and violence in the family. This scarcity of work also leads to seasonal migration of families from one part of the state to another, either from rural to rural, or rural to urban. The second wave appears when examinations results are announced. Afraid of the consequences, the not so academically inclined children run away from home. Those who face transitional problems in the new academic level also choose to run away from the suffocating and strangulating academic sphere.

Age Group Classifications

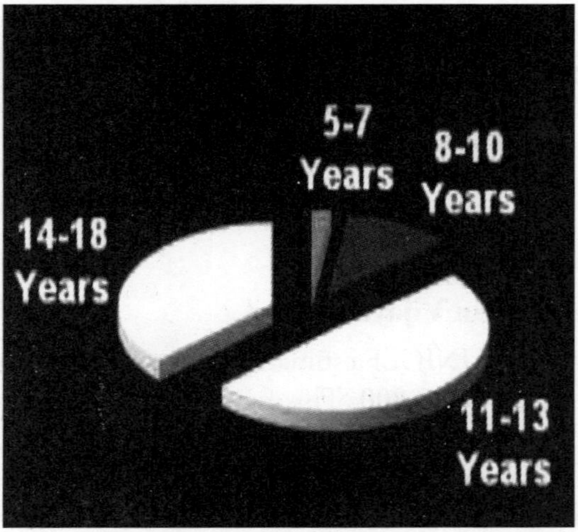

Source: Forum for Child Rights, Vijayawada

Gender Dimension of the Issue

About 96% of the children are boys and the remaining are girls. But, in recent times, observers state that the number of girl children arriving at the Vijayawada railway station is on the rise. One possible explanation for the present low turn-out among girls may be that girls are more vulnerable in the street than in homes. Hence, girls are likely to silently suffer the abuse and exploitation heaped upon them in their home environment rather than run away. The patriarchal system too may be playing the role of deterrent in the case of girls, because, once they run away, it would be difficult for them to be re-integrated into the family. The prejudice and suspicion created by the girl's behavior would create an indelible scar on her and on the family. Normalization and repatriation would be difficult. That is why most runaway girls never dream of going back home. If not rescued and rehabilitated, many of them enter into commercial sex work to secure a livelihood.

Place of Origin

About 85% of runaway children come from Andhra Pradesh itself. Only a marginal number of children come from other neighboring states such as Tamil Nadu, Karnataka, Maharashtra, Orissa and West Bengal. It could well be that the children find it difficult if not impossible to surmount the language barriers that exist from one state to another and thus decide to stay within their home territory.

This conclusion finds support in World Vision's collected data.

Another possibility could be that by the time they reach a city within the state they have been traced by the NGOs.The huge size of Andhra Pradesh with its 23 districts allows the child to wander within the state itself before he or she is traced.

Rehabilitation Work

To tackle these problems, the Village Service Trust has adopted two strategies:

Prevention

- ⇨ Preventing children from running away from their families.
- ⇨ Improving the quality of family life.
- ⇨ Contacting children who have recently run away as early as possible and providing opportunities for them to leave the street.

Protection

- ⇨ A Shelter Home
- ⇨ Education and Vocational Training
- ⇨ Medication
- ⇨ Advocacy Programs

These rescue and rehabilitation programs serve the needs of these children. They must be provided with a home, food, clothing and medical aid. They need a basic education and some vocational training. The education and training provided is aimed at making them literate and equipping them with some skills to find employment, or to start work on their own, and thus make a living. The objectives, nonetheless, go far beyond providing the assistance that simply allows these street children to fight another day. In fact, the mission is to transform the lives of these children, to return to them the ability to dream, to provide them with the means, the confidence, and the self-image they need to fully realize their potential, and to help them bloom into healthy, self-reliant individuals. Once their most basic needs are satisfied, a full rehabilitation requires that we give them back their childhood.

Rehabilitation

The government, international organizations and non-governmental organizations (NGOs) have taken several initiatives for the rehabilitation and education of street children and working children in India. The task is difficult and requires the full support of NGOs, social organizations, civil society, teachers, parents and other members of society.

Focal Problems and Opportunities

The city of Vijayawada has more than 18,000 to 20,000 street children and the more conservative estimate is that 12 to 18 new runaways arrive at the railway station every day. They are **roofless, rootless** and **rightless** providing the focal areas for the project to tackle.

Even though there are multiple players involved in the task of rescue and rehabilitation of street children, the number of children at large in the streets of Vijayawada is so huge and growing in such numbers daily. Hence, the project is imperative to address the issue.

The NGOs also have a centralized strategy for a decentralized problem. The proposed project will strive to tackle the issue through a combination of centralized and decentralized strategy.

In many ways the proposed project will differ significantly from the strategies of the established NGOs, and will empower the children to actively participate and personally engage in the process.

Capacities and Vulnerabilities

As the issue of street children became widespread, it attracted multiple players. There are several local NGOs involved in the rehabilitation of street children. They have formed a forum to establish a working-relationship among themselves and with Government Agencies. Presently, World Vision is one of the important members of this forum. To avoid duplication of services, the project will focus on certain vital spheres, where other NGOs are unable to do enough because of financial constraints and their ideological stance.

Contact Centers

Although street children are dispersed throughout the citythe programs and services presently run by NGOs are geographically concentrated. Hence, many children who do not stay in drop-in centers and shelter homes are left out of the program's reach.

To counter this ineffectiveness the project has established contact centers at street children-prone locations like railway stations, the market, bus terminals, commercial centers, and public parks, to bring them under the ambit of the program. These contact centers will serve as a launch pad for longer interventions like addiction recovery, vocational training, etc. Healthcare, non-formal education and recreational services will also be provided at these centers.

Vocational Skills/Job Placement Cell

The children who arrive at Vijayawada are usually unskilled, and as a result they end-up doing dehumanizing and hazardous jobs like rag-picking and cleaning railway bogeys, or dead-end jobs, like pulling rickshaws and cleaning tables in hotels, etc. Those who don't get any jobs resort to begging. Though providing education for these children would be an ideal solution, many harbor a deep seated revulsion to formal education.

Regrettably, in this era of sophisticated technology, being unskilled connotes powerlessness. Hence, to empower these children it is necessary to impart market-relevant vocational skills. All the NGOs involved in providing vocational training are presently providing outdated skills like screen printing, tailoring, drawing, carpentry, etc. The social worker's interaction with the children reveals that these skills do not help the children to earn an income which will truly make them independent. The project will address this issue by identifying and imparting market relevant skills to these street children in the area of like baking & making confectionary, catering, auto-mechanics, electrician, computer hardware and software, etc. The project will also arrange apprenticeships and provide job placements.

Micro-Enterprise Development/Income Generation Program

Because of their previous experience as child laborers, some of the children find working as an employee suffocating. They prefer to venture into the world of business and self-employment.

The Project will provide consultancy services and business-start-up capital to such aspirants. Those who are afraid of venturing into unchartered waters may be provided with income generation programs like producing & marketing consumer products. Economic Development Assistance (EDA) will be used as an instrument to achieve these goals.

Repatriation

One of the strategic blunders being committed by the NGOs presently involved in rehabilitating street children is that they invest so much of their limited resources in building sophisticated infrastructure in the form of buildings to accommodate the runaways, and then to keep these centers occupied they retain the children without repatriating them.

We acknowledge that these kinds of long-term interventions (famously called the "village model") are indeed required for those children who cannot be rehabilitated. But, it should not become an excuse to keep children away from their homes. Further, it immerses the staff of these NGOs in the business of administering "the village," instead of doing more outreach programs like rescue and repatriation. The Project will focus more on repatriating suitable cases after providing relief in short-stay homes. Those children that cannot be repatriated will be referred to institutions for long-term intervention.

Bridge Schools/Transit Schools

The Project will operate bridge-schools in the target areas to help street children originating from nearby slums in Vijayawada to assimilate into the school system. School dropouts in these target slums are often forced to work as child laborers, one of the pre-eminent causes for the incidence of street children.

Capacity Building of Stakeholders

There are several identified social groups, which have immediate contact/accessibility to street children and their groups. i.e., Railway porters, Policemen (Railway & Civil), Rickshaw Pullers, Auto-Rickshaw wallas, Commercial Sex Workers, etc. Apart from these, The Project will form its own child protection committee at vantage points in the city to monitor and safeguard street children. These stakeholders, and volunteers will conduct capacity building training on simple counseling, children's rights, in association with the other partners of the Child Rights Forum.

Participation & Leadership/Working Children Forum:

The lack of a credible platform to represent and advocate their issues negatively affects the interests of street children. Without any organized platform, the children find themselves powerless before the organized mafia (employers), and law enforcement. If we want to find a lasting solution to the problem of exploitation and abuse, these children should be organized, which would enable them to collectively voice their concerns and influence the policy making decisions. Further, this kind of organized forum will provide opportunities for the children to participate in the program and to extract accountability from non-government and government agencies, and will add to the sustainability of The Project as well.

Target Population Selection and Description

Children especially street and working children who are below 18 years old are the primary target group of The Project. But, as a part of a preventive strategy, The Project will also target the temporary settlement of migrant communities and slums, which also has a concentration of commercial sex workers.

Under the Convention on the Rights of the Child, children are entitled to all forms of rights. Street children are denied the right to shelter, right to food, right to health care services, right to protection, right to development and right to recreation. Keeping in mind the "best interest of the child," The Project will address all these issues.

Seasonal Dimension of the Issue

Though the influx of street children is perennial in nature, it varies from season to season. Mostly the children arrive at the end of the agricultural seasons and when the academic examination results are announced.

Each and every year, the first wave of street children starts when the agricultural operation comes to a grinding halt; it makes the landless laborers redundant and unemployed, leading to the vicious cycle of scarcity, deprivation and violence in the families. Also it leads to seasonal migration of families from one part of the state to other parts either from rural to rural or rural to urban. The second wave of arrival starts when the examinations results are announces, afraid of the consequences the not so academically inclined children run away from home. Those who face transitional problems in the new academic level also choose to run away from the suffocating and strangulating academic sphere.

NGOs and Social Work Agencies working among Street Children in Vijayawada

SKCV

SKCV (Street Kids' Community Villages) is a project for homeless young people in Vijayawada, Southern India. Founded in 1984 by

Manihara, a family friend, it is home to more than 150 boys, girls and young adults who would otherwise be living rough on the streets.

Bosco Seva Kendra: De-Addiction Centre for Street Children, Vijayawada

This organization works towards the Eradication of Child, Bonded Labor and Rehabilitation of Street / Working Children and School dropouts.

Nava Jeevan Bala Bhavan, Vijayawada

The Don Bosco Community established Navajeevan in 1989, at the invitation of the Municipal Corporation of Vijayawada, to rescue and rehabilitate street children. Those children, who cannot find their homes for various reasons, are encouraged to choose from options for rehabilitation - regular education/training in various trades and other life skills which would inculcate in them self-esteem and confidence to be self-reliant.

Care and Share

Care and Share has been involved in the rescue and rehabilitation of street children since 1995. In 1996 it set up Sweet Home, a rescue home for boys. In November 1997 it set up Ginny's Home, a rescue home for girls, and in March 1999 it started Tote's Home, its second home for young girls. In May 1999, it started building Daddy's Home, a permanent residence for destitute children. In 2005, it began construction at Butterfly Hill, its new campus for street children. More than 800 children are presently sheltered in Care and Share.

Forum for Child Rights

Forum for Child Rights, Vijayawada was set up under the presidency of the honorable mayor. It was officially inaugurated on August 14, 1997, the eve of the Golden Jubilee of India's Independence. The Forum includes NGOs, activists, well-wishers and philanthropists in the city. The Forum's objectives can be summed up in its motto: "Make Vijayawada a Child Friendly City."

Chapter 5

Data Collection, Data Analysis and Case Studies

Introduction

Data has been collected from World Vision offices from their records and analyzed. This data is mainly gathered from the period of two months, January & February 2011. A few case studies are studied by the researcher personally and analyzed under the light of office records and field observation.

In the month of Jan 2011 there were 21 runaway children identified by World Vision office staff from various points such as the railway station, bus station, signal points, cinemas, theaters, etc. Apart from the World Vision there are many such organizations helping, but here we will take into consideration the World Vision context only.

Runaway children are identified from the period Jan 2011 to Feb 2011.

There are 52 children identified from the period Jan 2011 to Feb 2011, 31 in the month of Jan & 19 in the month of Feb 2011.

Gender analysis

Among them

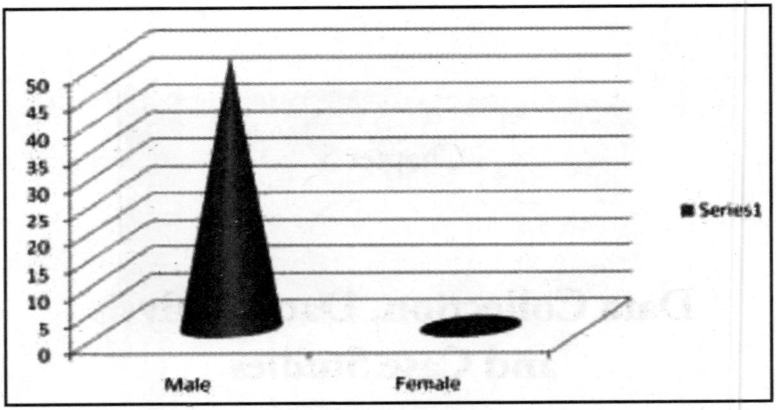

Male	50
Female	2
Total	**52**

This data gives an impression to the reader that the male rate is very high compared to female rate. In this context, one of the World Vision staff, Mr. Divakar informed me in my interview with him that "the female cases are very rare and mostly we get male cases in finding out the runaway cases."[59] There may be many reasons for this, including that females are scared to go out from the home. In fact, parents are also conscious for the female children. Usually the male children are crazy for movies and they long for freedom which may be the reason for this epidemic. In fact, the reading on this subject also informed me that "the typical street kid is a male between 11 and 13 years of age; a majority of them hail from other towns and villages within Andhra; most are Hindu and belong to castes that the government designate as 'backward.'[60] All the identified children are properly taken care of and they are counseled properly with the skilled counseling techniques. After the initial counseling the interested children are sent back to their home which they called 'Repatriation.' Those who are not interested to go home are sent to the existing child care centers and home.

During these two months identified children's placement follows.

Home wise placements

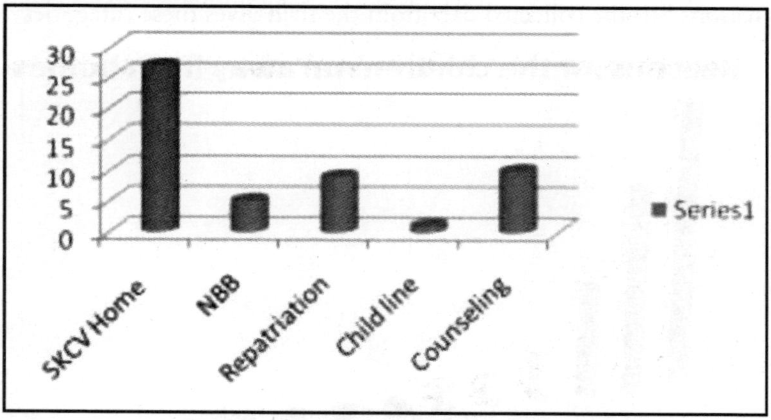

SKCV Home	27
NBB	5
Repatriation	9
Child line	1
Counseling	10
Total	**52**

The above data informs the reader that SKCV home might have a good tie with World Vision office because a good number of kids are handed over to them. In fact, SKCV has been working in the city which has been founded in 1984 by Manihara, a family friend; it is home to over 150 boys, girls and young adults who would otherwise be living rough on the streets.

Reasons for leaving their home

The careful analyses of the collected data inform the reader that there are several reasons for children leaving home. The main reasons among them are Chronic poverty, Parents' irresponsibility, Deaf & Dumb, Physical & Mental disability, Orphans/Semi orphan/Step mother or father, Lack of knowledge on parenting skills, Peer group pressure, Forced child labor/Bonded child labor. There may be some other reasons but the collected data from the field gives these categories

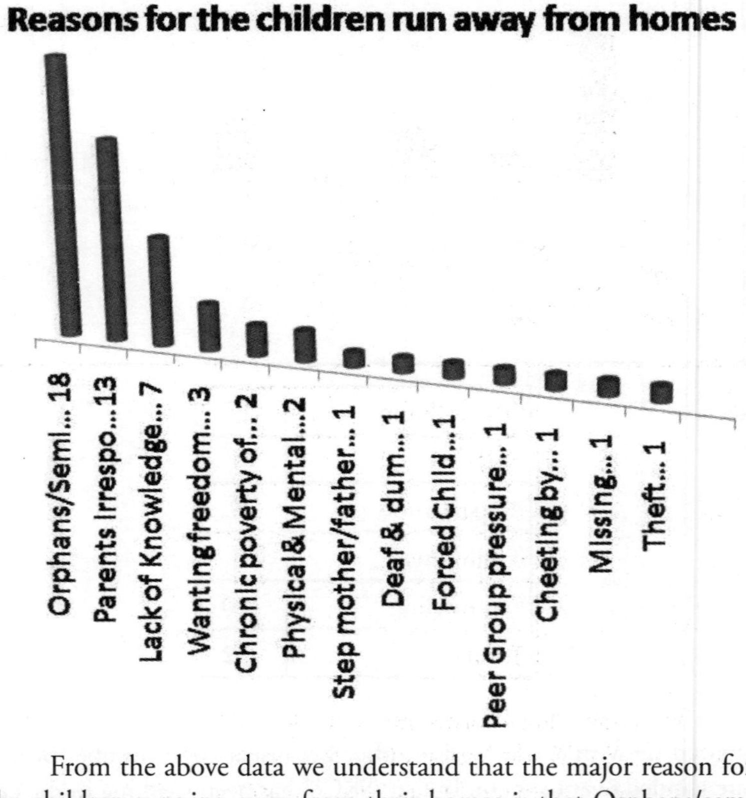

From the above data we understand that the major reason for the children running away from their homes is that Orphans/semi orphan/step mother. This is one of the significant observations that in Vijayawada the orphans' rate is high. There may be several reasons for this epidemic but it shows that the family system has some problem due to the societal changes. One of my interviews with World Vision staff mentioned that "when the children do not get love from the parents they get disturbed and that may cause them to run away from their home."[61] Family is a unit in which the children enjoy the love from parents and from other members of the family but in these days the family system has been damaged due to societal changes. As the result the children in the families are not able to enjoy love and acceptance. This needs serious attention by the social agencies...

Runaway Children Identified District Wise

Krishna district	15
Guntur district	12
East Godavari	4
Other states	4
Visakhapatnam district	3
West Godavari district	3
Not informed	3
Prakasam district	2
Nellore district	2
Rangareddy	2
Warangal	1
Kurnool district	1
Adilabad	0
Nizamabad district	0
Karimnagar	0
Medak	0
Nalgonda	0
Mahbubnagar	0
Khammam	0
Hyderabad	0
Anantapur district	0
Kadapa district	0
Chittoor district	0
Srikakulam district	0
Vizianagaram district	0
Total	**52**

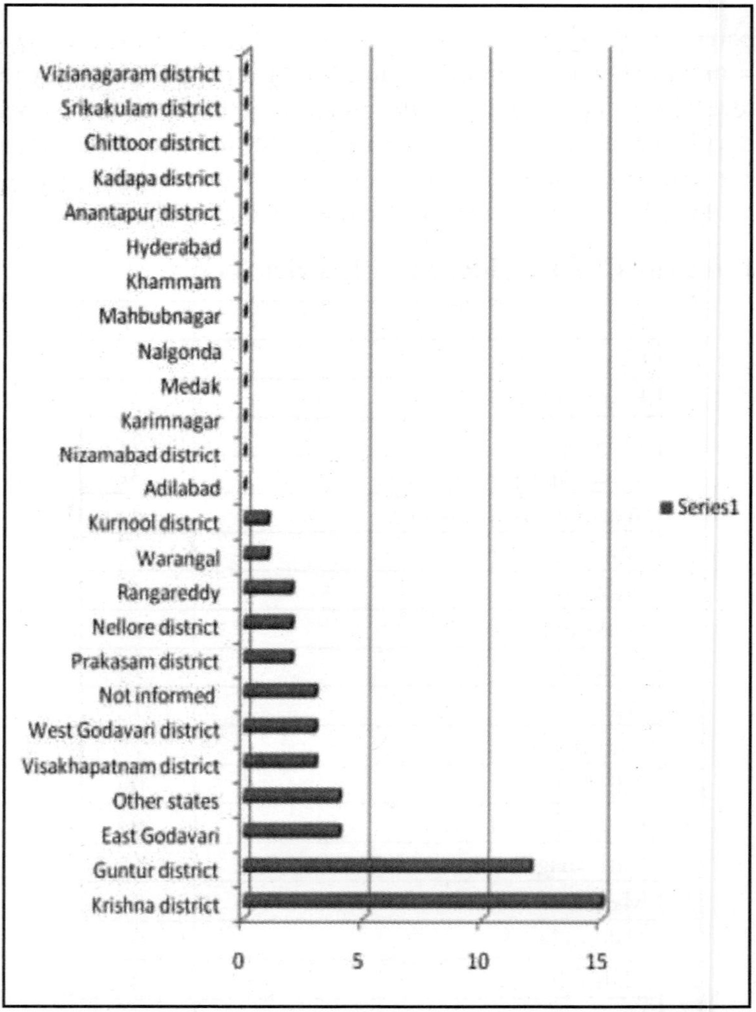

The runaway children who were traced in the city of Vijayawada belong to different districts of the state as well as a few of them are traced from other states also. The significant observation from the most of the identified children belong to Krishna & Guntur Districts which inform us that most of the runaway children try to settle with in the nearby towns and cities. During the initial stage, the runaway children can be traced near by the towns and cities. Parents who miss their child can immediately start searching nearby the city and town.

We can educate the parents that they should immediately inform the police at nearby cities and towns so that the child can be traced. This phenomenon may not be true with all the cases because quite a number of cases have come from other districts such as Kurnool, Ranga Reddy, Vishakhapatnam, etc., for my surprise there is no child from the head quarter of the state Hyderabad. This gives me an impression that children always move from village to city and from city to mega city. Since Hyderabad is a mega city, kids may not move out from that mega city to smaller cities.

In this context, I assume that city has such an attracting power that it attracts all segments of people. The kids also try to run away from the smaller town to bigger city. This may be the reason that most of our Indian cities are filled with these street children. Thus, the project work for the rehabilitation should be established in the cities that to nearby Railway or Bus stand.

The Age Factor

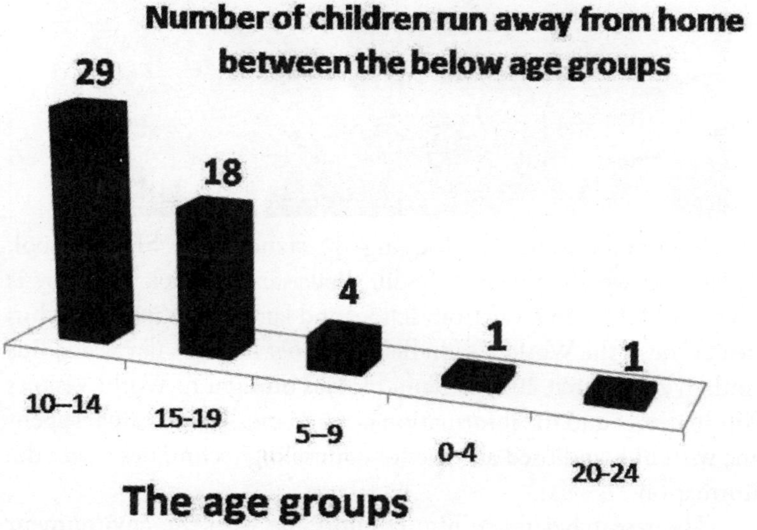

From the above table, we can understand that it is mostly between ages 10 and 14 that children run away from home. This is the most vulnerable age due to peer pressure and other factors such as the media. This gives us an indication that the parents need to be educated that they should be very careful with children once they turn 10. The child's rationality and the craving for love and acceptance may tempt him to run away from home. In order to help the child, the parents should understand the child's need of love, acceptance and respect. The child should receive his parents' love so that he grows up in a peaceful atmosphere.

Case Studies

Case Study of Nageswara Rao; 12 yrs

Nageswara Rao was studying 8th standard at SPH School, Mallavaram which is near to Podili, Prakasam District. This boy is 12 years old. He ran away from school and landed in Vijayawada bus stand. One of the World Vision field staff met him at Vijayawada Bus stand on 29th March 2011 at 9am. He was brought to World Vision's drop-in center and the information came to me. The researcher spent time with him and used all types of counseling techniques to get the information.

The researcher made him comfortable with the environment in the drop-in center and he got the confidence and started trusting me to interact. He took a bath and the World Vision office gave him a new dress because his dress became very dirty. After some time of rest and food he revealed his brother Chittibabu's mobile number.

The researcher called his brother and found out that he ran away from home.

The researcher understood from my interaction with the child and with his family members that a lack of love and care is the main reason for this case. Since he has no father, he has been longing for love and acceptance from family members, but his mother always neglects him. In fact, his two brothers and mother always ill-treat him and he is forced to work while he is still young enough to go to school.

His brother sent one of his uncles from Guntur at 5pm of the same day and the child was repatriated safely.

One significant observation I made from this study is that this boy is good in his studies, because the researcher tested him to read and write English, which he did very well. In fact he was 2nd in his school results. If World Vision would not have traced him he would have lost his bright future.

Case Study of a Slum nearby Vijayawada Bus Stand

Along with World Vision Staff the researcher visited a slum near the Vijayawada bus stand. His eyes are opened to the reality of poverty and struggles of human misery. The living condition is extremely horrible and there are nearly 100 huts without proper roof and basic facilities. The researcher interacted with kids and ladies who are available over there. All the males of the slum go for chain, pins, etc. selling business in the running trains and the ladies and the small kids go for egging in the trains.

In fact begging is the main profession for these people. The kids are beautiful but they are harassed and helpless. The researcher interacted with a few kids who are in this profession. In fact they are happy and they don't want to go to school.

The researcher interacted and interviewed above lady whose story inspired him a lot. She is married now and she has three children but still she continues her begging. She looks good and no one thinks that she is in this profession. In fact, her two brothers have studied well and they are not in this profession but still she continues. The researcher found the reasons for this because she is habituated to this profession. While she was very small her life started in the train especially passenger trains from Vijayawada to Gudivada and Tenali routes. Her parents are drama & dance players by profession but due to the extreme poverty her parents started begging in the trains and this girl was also forced into this business. As a small kid she started begging and continues till date. She plays harmonium and sings songs and her small daughter collects the begging money. She is forcing her two daughters also into this trap. We counseled her to send her kids to school and we are in contact with this slum to help the kids.

Case Study of a Children home, ARUNODAYA

The researcher visited Arunodaya Street Children home which is runned by Church of South India (CSI). The Street children in this home are rugged ones, who have all sorts of habits. There is a lady who takes care of them, but the home is not properly planned to rehabilitate these children. Most of the children are somewhat grown-up teenage boys. They roam the street whole day and come to the center at night for shelter and food. The center gives food to the kids and some support for their handy works but there is no constructive rehabilitation strategy. The researcher interacted with a few boys and played with them so that they gave the needed information. Most of these boys go for catering job and earn a little to spend on the Bazaar. Their life is on the Bazaar and they don't like to settle, even if they get some help from the people and organization they like to spend it leisurely and then again want to live like Bazaar children. Since they don't have proper care and strategic planning of rehabilitation they just live like that and move from city to city.

Case Study of another Children home, AMMA VODI

The researcher was very much excited by observing this "Amma Vodi" children rehabilitation center at Vijayawada. The center is very strategically working to liberate the kids holistically. There are nearly 100 kids both boys and girls in the center. The significant observation from this center is that the kids are properly taken care of and they are getting good education and over all developmental projects. This is the first time the researcher observed that the kids in a rehabilitation center are going for higher studies like B.Tech, MA etc., the researcher interviewed two of the Bachelor of Technology (B.Tech) students in the center and was surprised to see their growth. The kids in the center call the manager of the center as "Amma," a Telugu word for Mother. She is like a mother in her relations and concern over the kids. The home has been contributing a significant contribution to the City of Vijayawada in the context of street children.

Case Study of Ravi

Ravi ran away from home when he was of seven years. He has one elder brother and one elder sister at "Khammam" a nearby town in Andhra Pradesh. He is the youngest sibling. His father died in his early age and mother worked hard in the neighboring house to meet the needs of the family for survival. Ravi left home, after he robbed his brother's money Rupees 700/-. He arrived Vijayawada Railway station and it was his base. He commuted in trains east and west. He cleaned the coach floors and begs for his survival. He was addicted to smoking, snatching and alcoholic solutions. He ate the left overs found in the dust bins of the Railway platform and used the thrown out cigar bits.

World vision staff Mr. Pragnan Kumar CDC met him & counseled him at Vijayawada railway station. With the consistent efforts of World Vision initiative, he started reducing the intake of alcohol and smoking. World Vision staffs treat RAVI AS a child OF GOD and nurtured the good habits and instilled hope of fullness of life with dignity, peace and joy.

He was supported to get rid of emotional barriers and he slowly improved to become a normal child. World Vision helped him to have proper shelter and other living needs at SKCV children trust.

At the SKCV shelter, Ravi has good fellowship with other children, and is obedient and helpful. World Vision helps hundreds of ran away children like Ravi to find the right life path and serve the best to have Life with all its Fullness.

Case Study of Kylash

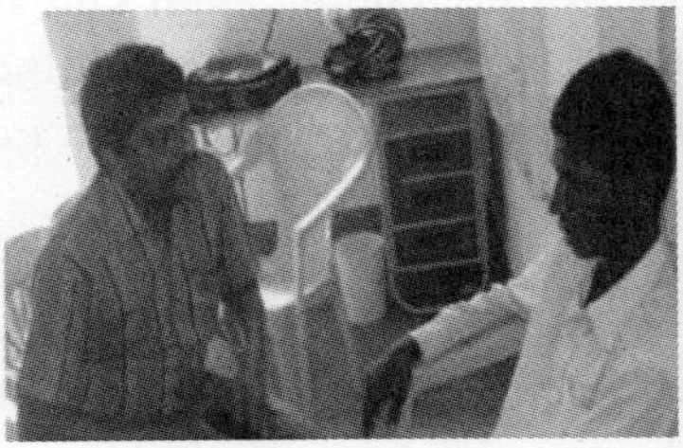

Kylash was found at the signal point in the city of Vijayawada at Benj Circle point. One of the World Vision staff Mr. Anand traced him and brought him to the drop-in center for rehabilitation. The researcher was given the privilege to interact with and counsel him.

The boy is nearly 16 years old and he speaks only Oria, the language of Orissa state. Since, he understood a little bit of Hindi, the researcher did his best to communicate with him but it did not work out. One of the observations of this boy is that he is not a lost case as such but he is away from home to search some work for his survival.

Lack of education and poverty are the main reasons for such boys. Since he is an adult and not able to speak any language apart from Oria, one of the staff from Nava Jeevan came to the drop-in center and took him to Nava Jeevan child care center. Nava Jeevan gave him some shelter and are taking care of him.

Case Study of Seema

A child named Seema ran away from Nagpur to Hyderabad. In her journey the train stopped in Vijayawada. The ticket collector asked for the ticket and immediately she ran from the train and came to the platform. Child Line staff approached her and Mr. Ramesh did counseling and put her in an observation home.

She revealed her case to the staff. She is not literate. She hasn't felt her home is a secure place for her to stay. She noticed illegal activities are taking place in her house. My mother is earning Rs 500/- per day, said Seema .She felt shy to reveal her mother's profession, her face was pale and sorrowful when she shared family things to staff. She is 10 years old.

Now she is staying in an observation home playing with children, willing to study, and she know only Hindi. "Staff said at least 15 days it took to see laugh on her face". We want to call the mother for counseling but she has not given a correct address; we are hoping for reunification.

Most Significant Change Story

I would like to share the transformation, which has taken place in the lives of children through the collective efforts of World Vision.

The situation of some of the girls in the project was worse but now they became role models to other children. During our survey, we found that most of the girls in the poor families were becoming child laborers to support their families financially. Their poverty becomes a great hurdle to these children in continuing their education, though they have keen interest in education. However, their family conditions were not favorable to them to reach their goals. This situation disturbs the children, and they are unable to continue their studies. The project has identified this problem and has given priority to address this issue. We have counseled the parents and helped the children to continue their education from the point of its discontinuation. We have searched for alternative methods to continue their studies and found that professional and technical trainings are better for these children to reach their goals.

It is our great pleasure to share some success stories among the girls who have gone through these professional courses. Their ambition has made them to stand on their own two feet. We can see the following success stories as models....

"I was at cross of the roads; I did not know where to go. But, now I have reached my goal and feeling very happy" this voice is from the girl who has to spend the time joyfully. But, she worked in labor quarry. Now she is released from that situation and spending her time very happily. She is a role model to many girls. Her life style in her own words....

I am Nagamani; we are from Gadhireddynagar slum in Rajahmundry. My father is a Lorry driver in a Quarry. Mother also used to work in quarry. At present she is at house. Before you know about my past and me, you have to know about my family. There is a lot of difference between my past life and present life. I was at the cross roads; I did not know where I was going. Nevertheless, presently I reached my goal. I am in seventh heaven. My family was very poor. My house-a two room house-has been built with the Government's help. My father is a drunkard. He used to spend all that he earns on drinking liquor. Mother used to take care of the problems at home. She did not have capacity to bring up her children. So my brother was adopted to my grandfather who was in Gokavaram Village. My elder sister was married with the person from whom we borrowed money. When I was in 10th class, I used to study joyfully. But, at that time there broke out a big fight in the family.

My married sister came to my home with her two children as she could not bear with her husband. As my father did not take care about my family, I had to go to labor work to get food. I could not forget that day when I was sent forcefully to work. That day I cried a lot and I prayed God. Mother, sister and I worked very hard for the family to survive. I spent many sleepless nights. But, I could not imagine myself without education. So, finally when I passed 10th class my joy knew no bounds, but still I faced so many problems to join in the college. My parents could not support me. They scolded and thrashed me. Finally, I thought there was no other way so I took poison to commit suicide but by the grace of God I survived.

Child Protection Unit members of my community understand my deep desire for education. They spoke to my parents and introduced me to World Vision for necessary help. The CPU Committee met the World Vision's volunteer Miss Phoebe Ratna who works in Ramdaspeta slum and explained my case. She understood my problem and helped me to join in Prathibha Vocational College in Medical Lab Technician Course. She also bought a uniform for me with her own money and encouraged me a lot. One of my cousins (brother) helped me to buy books. With that support I studied very interestingly by walking 2 km daily from my house to college. During holidays, I worked in cloth shops and factories and helped my family financially. Even then my parents warned me to go to work daily to earn more money. However, my burning desire to study made me strong and I did not listen to their words. I passed in 1st grade but I was very keen on joining in a nursing course. Though my strong interest in education coupled with good results in exams changed the attitude of my parents towards education, they could not spend money on my studies. In this situation, World Vision India played a vital role in my life.

World Vision's staff spoke to my parents and convinced them to send me for higher courses. And my slum CPU also has taken a special care on me. They also encouraged two more girls along with me and joined us in Staff nursing course by getting financial help from World Vision towards the fees.

I will not forget World Vision India till my last breath. I was in cloud nine and was extremely happy when World Vision gave me such timely support. As a result of their kind help only I could get into Mother Teresa School of Nursing for "staff nurse" course. I studied very hard for three and half years. When all other students of my class were going to home happily during the holidays between I used to feel very sad of my family situation. But, World Vision helped me to complete my course and I passed in 1st grade with good percentage. Due to this reason, I could become a proud employee of a big hospital in my town called "Sai Hospitals". It really enhanced my self-esteem in the society, and made me to support my family financially. I cannot forget the World Vision's role in my life. It changed my life. Now my parents take pride in my achievements. Hence, we are very much thankful to God and to World Vision India.

Nagamani now has become a role model to many children in her community. Her life changed her parents' attitude towards education. Now, they have decided to give good education to their younger daughters who are studying in high school at present. Nagamani is still waiting to achieve her goal that she wants to go to USA and get experience, to be in a better position and wants to help many girls who are like her. May we bless her to achieve still greater success in her life.

Case Study of Mallidi Krishna Kumari

This is about Mallidi Krishna Kumari who is from a poor family living in "timber depot" community. Fishing is their main occupation. She failed in 10th class. Her parents cannot afford her studies. Therefore, she is at home without any work. She spends her time by doing domestic work. World Vision's CDC identified her and counseled her and motivated her to rewrite the 10th class exams. But, her parents refused and said that nobody from their caste could go for higher studies.

After coming to know about the Indira Kranthi Scheme (A government scheme for youth development) through World Vision they agreed to enroll her in the course called hotel management after several efforts. With her parent's permission, and with her interest, she attended hospitality course (Hotel Management). World Vision also helped her by providing auto fares so that she can regularly attend the classes. She has utilized the course very well. After the successful completion of the course she was selected for a job in Hyderabad. Now she is working very happily.

"My heartfelt thanks to World Vision for providing a golden opportunity for my daughter to do the job though no one in my caste is doing any job" – Suryarao, Father of Krisna Kumari.

Case Study of Ramanujam

This is about Ramanujam Prameela Devi. She failed in one subject in 10th class. Moreover, when she was idle at home, she was contacted by World Vision's staff and enrolled into skill training center run by World Vision. During her course, she was given information about Indira Kranthi scheme. She and her parents were motivated by our staff and admitted in hospitality (Hotel Management) course. Project helped her for auto fare to regularly attend the classes. She utilized the provided opportunity very well.

While she was studying the same course, she was selected by a company through campus interview and joined in the job related to the course. After two months she wants to rewrite her 10th class exams. Presently she is working in Hotel Atidi at Hyderabad.

Case Study of Sridevi

Sridevi lost her father. Her mother was doing casual labor. As her mother was earning very little, Sridevi was under the care of her brother and sister- in- law. She failed 10th class. Project staff saw her sitting idle at home, and motivated her to join a skill training center run by World Vision where she can learn some skills for her better future. After joining this center only she realized that she was losing her precious time by just sitting idle at home.

She completed the course in skill training center. During the course of time she was motivated to re write the subject failed in 10th class. This time also she could not succeed but she didn't lose her interest in education. Through the counseling given to her during her skill training, she joined marketing skills course in Ready's lab under Indira Kranthi scheme with the help of World Vision. During the course, she was selected in campus interview and got a job at Hyderabad. But, she could not be there for a long time as the weather was not suitable to her. She left it and came back home. Within a few days she got a job in Rajahmundry with the skills she learned through World Vision in glass painting and making toys.

These are the few stories of children who have gone through professional and technical trainings. We can see a lot of transformation in their lives and many other children are motivated to continue their studies because of these success stories.

Case Study of Srilekha

Srilekha 18 years an orphan found at railway platform at the age of 5 years, was caught by a volunteer and put in a shelter home Ammavodi. She didn't know her parents, relatives and any one in the world. When she grows up she knows that she was an orphan. She knows only the mother and father of the home and the number of children who called her sister and Srelekha also owning & calling them as her brothers and sisters, now she is studying B.Sc., Nursing 1st year. In the last month our staff counseled her through green bag tool given by (SGM) Scripture Gift Mission. At that time, she opened her feelings and weeping about her condition nobody is there to share about my feelings, if I have my mother she knows my needs according to my age, but this counseling changed my attitude towards positive thinking. In a recent visit, Mr. L. R. Joshi explained the importance of education and goal of the future settlement and she got inspired and challenged to complete her studies and settle in life after that to get married and then to serve the children like me there are many of them who need service. But, she needs proper counseling and assistance to complete her studies. In turn others were transformed through her life she will be the model to many.

When she attended the Green Bag counseling, she learned that God loves her. She felt very happy to listen the stories of Jesus and his love for the children. According to her words, she was filled with joy to know that Jesus loves her.

At the time of the counseling there were no answers for many questions, because she does not have anybody and no experience to share. She just smiled and showed a blank face. But, with the green bag counseling she learned that God is in the mother's place and cares for her. Because of that only she was saved from the platform by the volunteer and now she is able to do the Nursing course.

She expressed thanks to God and wanted to become a useful weapon in the hands of God to serve many children in future.

Case Study of Shaik Gowsiya

According to Gowsiya, she lost her father in early childhood. She was the only child of her parents. Her mother had illegal contact with another man after his death and had a child. But, the man had lot of horrific habits, he also used to beat both mother and child. One day, he made an attempt to kill her mother. She escaped but lost both of her hands and went to the hospital for treatment. Gowsiya saw the incident and became estranged for two months. While her mother was under medication in the hospital, she attempted suicide and died right in the hospital. After that, Gowsiya tried to stay at her sister's house but was turned away by them.

She decided to leave them and got on a train; she reached Khajipet in 3 splits of the journey. Then she came to Vijayawada. The Railway Police identified her and she was sent to an observation home SETHU. After two months, she escaped from the home and tried to go back to her mother town. She was found at Auto Nagar gate by a rag picker. She doesn't want to go back to SETHU due to the fear of other children's annoyance. She got attracted and willingly went along with the rag picker at Auto Nagar where the family stays at a temporary shelter, and then she was shifted to another sister's house at VAMBAY Colony. One of the staff of World Vision, brought into my notice about this child. I visited the child and her caretaker's family, counseled them and made arrangements to observe the child and her keepers by a local pastor's family at VAMBAY colony.

Success Story

In another case, a vulnerable child who was the eldest daughter of a family was counseled as she was ready to leave her parents because she was not interested in studies. Both her parents were motivated with positive counseling and willingly they send her into a residential care for her better future.

In Gowsiya case also, she was motivated and willingly she came to our day care center on Sept. 2, 2010. After that we contacted a local NGO called "AMMA ODI" and enrolled the child on 13 Sept. 2010 for residential care. Again the child ran away after 3 days and was found in VAMBAY colony. She was again counseled and arrangements were made for her regular and constant observation by our CBO/FBO/Staff/Volunteer.

Chapter 6

Major Findings and Recommendations

Major Findings of the Study

The basic issues of the street and working children are to protect them from abuse in the cities through preventive and protective measures. The preventive measures require mass awareness of society, parents and the children, whereas the protective measures include provision of survival strategies, security, psychological support and educational and vocational skills in the cities to these children as otherwise the children are susceptible to drugs, inhalants and alcoholic addictions and sexual abuse which ultimately forces them to work for mafia and crime rings. These children are also prone to occupational hazards leading to diseases and accidents, which affect their lives, limbs, psyche and total development. International pressure and support from UN agencies, sustained movement generated by NGOs, judicial activism and concerted efforts from the National Human Rights Commission has contributed significantly to draw government attention to address the street and working children concerns confronting the society. In this direction several legislative measures and field based action plans have been operationalized. The culmination of these efforts resulted in the adoption of the National Child Labor Project (NCLP) in the endemic areas of the country having child labor in hazardous occupations.

In this context, World Vision of India should continue to raise its voice to defend the rights and privileges of the street kids.

Since several national and international donor agencies also support NGOs in providing rehabilitation and education programs to the children. Child line service is also activated in several cities to provide immediate referral services to the vulnerable children.

The problems of street and working children are exogenous to the situations of metropolitan cities. We have to look into the socio-culture situation of the families in their native places while dealing with the problem. A significant proportion of the families of street and working children living in the cities have migrated from the rural areas hoping to get absorbed in the economic productive process in the cities. But, most of them end up working in the low-paid unskilled jobs in the unorganized sector. The earnings are meager, which is not at all sufficient for them to maintain their families, especially in the cities where the cost of living is high. They end up pushing their children to fend for themselves and their families.

The study indicates that, the magnitude of out-of-school children are in the surveyed selected slums, especially near by Bus stand slum. These children are engaged either in petty jobs earning a meager amount or are simply wandering aimlessly on the streets because of their parents' lack of awareness or indifferent attitude of the civil society to give them proper direction and guidance. These children are also susceptible to various diseases owing to their stay in unhygienic environments for most of the time. Therefore, these children are in need of health awareness, proper nutrition and educational opportunities.

The study points out that a significant proportion of "of-the street" category of children usually succumb to drugs, inhalant and alcoholic addictions, or sexual assaults or are convicted for petty theft and put in the remand homes by the police if not protected by the society. These children are also susceptible to societal and police abuse. In order to protect themselves, they end up playing into the hands of crime rings.

These children also face the problems of scattered resources in the cities, as they are unaware of the existence of several agencies providing support to them. However, children were supportive of the Child Line service introduced in several cities and they feel it helps them to make them aware of the existing support in the cities. Most of the children are not in favor of institutionalizing the services for them, rather they want these services should be available in an integrated form on the streets, so that they can live independently and at the same time utilize these facilities.

The majority of NGOs surveyed do provide non-formal education to the street and working children but only 25 per cent of these NGOs provide day/night shelters, healthcare, clothing, and vocational skills to the street and working children. The number of such NGOs/institutions having residential homes and other day/night stay facilities are less compared to the requirements of these children in the city of Vijayawada. Moreover, the respondents also felt that shelter, toilet and bath facilities were highly inadequate and in an appalling condition in some of the shelter homes and drop-in centers. Even the NGOs receiving funds from the Ministry of Social Justice and Empowerment to provide shelter and other protective measures for the street category of children were not providing qualitative services.

Drug de-addiction and healthcare for the children was available only in a few centers. Shelter homes for girls were minimal in the city; with the result that runaway girls end up facing sexual assaults and other harassment. The infrastructure of the non-formal education provided by the NGOs is inadequate to cater to the needs of street and working children in the urban areas.

The Government of India must adopt the 83rd Constitutional Amendment at the earliest recognizing elementary education as a fundamental right for all Indian citizens. Formation of a nodal agency to converge various activities related to the rehabilitation and education programs for street and working children by central and state governments under various ministries. This will reduce duplication of activities and help in utilizing the activities and support judiciously and effectively.

Non-formal education and other alternative education programs should be viewed as a supplementary support for the formal education system in the initial stages. Ultimately, mainstreaming of all children in formal education is the ultimate goal and NGOs should act as pressure groups to improve quality of education in the formal schools.

Development of a uniform core content of curriculum along with area-specific curriculum and identification of area-specific teaching-learning materials.

A teacher-learning guide with details of methods of teaching, methodology for preparation of lessons for teachers and monthly targets of curriculum to be completed by the teachers should be prepared by the committee in consultation with the teachers from successful NGOs.

From this research a number of short-term recommendations emerge:

- There is need for co-ordination of responses to street children's rights.
- There is need to conduct a best practices survey or study of responses to street children and to share this with all stakeholders.
- A process could be initiated through child-welfare forum to review existing legislation on children and how these could be strengthened.
- There is need for research to be conducted to fill the information gap on the effects of street environments on child development.
- The World Vision of India needs to seriously consider re-deploying its welfare departments into development departments. This would mean that the Departments of Child Welfare and Social Welfare would focus more on child and social development. The fact that it is much more expensive to "cure" than to "prevent" cannot be overstated.

- Many of the organizations working in the area of street children have been in existence for a couple of years. In the long-term it could be beneficial for these to have a capacity assessment in order for intervening around NGO, CBO or organizational capacity-building.
- Community mobilization should be a priority in ensuring duty-bearers are "keeping their promise" to children of AP, including street children.

Other Recommendations[62]

Most of the mentioned recommendations under this heading are taken from the World Visions mission practices and its documents.

Project Partners Analysis

This project would like to closely work with the following organization at the grass root level as they play key role in the implementation of the activities.

NGOs

As the issue of street children became widespread, it attracted multiple players into the scenario. There are several local NGOs involved in the rehabilitation of street children. They have formed a forum to establish a working-relationship among themselves and with Government Agencies. Presently, World Vision is one of the important members of this forum. To avoid duplication of services, the project will focus on certain vital spheres, where other NGOs are not doing adequately enough because of financial constraints / ideological stance. At the same time there will be develop coordination among these NGOs to meet the common goal of the project.

Children's Clubs: (In all target slums & contact centers)

1. To ensure enhance their participation in social life
2. To educate children on child rights
3. To foster mutual-help among children
4. To provide opportunity to develop their talents/skills
5. To engineer behavioral changes among children

Street/Working Children Forum: (Will be run by the street/working children & for the street/working children) to represent & take up the cause of street/working children

- To monitor NGO/government programs
- To forge an alliance at the national level
- To foster relationship with police to remove mistrust

Child Protection Committees

Apart from the Children's Forums, there is no watch dog like mechanism inside the city to identify vulnerable children, violations against the children and to address the issue. The law enforcing machineries are either inaccessible or insensitive to such violations. Hence, the project will strive to form Child Protection Committees at street children prone areas like railway station, market, bus terminal, commercial centers, public parks, pilgrimage places, etc. to monitor, guide and safeguard children. The committee will serve as a watch dog to monitor the violations.

Detailed Implementation Plan Narrative Contact Visits

The children, if rescued immediately after they land in railway stations can be rehabilitated & repatriated with much ease. But, one they enter into streets, they learn the tricks of the trade and under the peer group pressure will learn many harmful habits which are hard to give up. Further, street children gangs gets involved in many illegal activities like drug-peddling and waiting in the wings to catch the new one in order to increase the size of their group. Anti-social elements, who are misusing small children for begging, are also looking for new children. These organized mafia rent out children for begging for an attractive amount on daily basis.

Hence, rescuing them immediately holds the key for the success of the program. Hence, the project will have systematic & sustained contact visit to rescue the children

Contact Centers

As mentioned earlier, street children are dispersed throughout the city and many children refuse even to come to a drop-in center. For these children, the project will establish contact centers at street children prone areas to keep in touch with them. Non-formal education, recreational facilities and Medicare will be provided in these centers. Children Clubs will be formed among the children attending these centers and each center will be monitored by a Child Protection Committee formed in that area. These centers will also serve as a strategic outpost to build relationship with stakeholders and street children.

Short-Stay Home

The rescued children will be immediately admitted in the short-stay home, where the immediate needs of the children like shelter, food, clothing, hygiene, recreation, Medicare and counseling will be met. Shelter will also have a non-formal education center and family counseling center. After assessing the viability of reunion with the family, the children will be repatriated.

If the circumstances do not favor repatriation, children will be referred to full-time institutions (famously called model villages) run by other NGOs, i.e., CARE&SHARE, NAVA JEEVAN BALA VIKAS, SKCV, etc., for long term intervention. Vijayawada receives only a small number of girls per year and soon after rescuing these girls will be referred to those residential-institutions exclusively built to accommodate girls.

Drop-In Centers (Night Shelter Home)

Many street children find the orderly & systematic life practiced in Shelter-Homes/Institutions very monotonous/oppressive and suffocating. Because, exactly from the orderly & monotonous life of child labor and suffocating & oppressive family environment, desperately they ran away in search of freedom. Hence, many continue to prefer a life on the street. But, street life is very unsafe and children are very vulnerable at the hands of adults. Hence, the project will operate a Drop-In center at a vantage location to provide night shelter to children.

Family & Individual Counseling/Medicare

Counseling is expected to play a vital role in engineering behavioral changes among the children and their families. Many children suffer post-traumatic syndrome as a result of the abuse, violence & exploitation above all breach of trust they suffered at the hands of their immediate family members. To overcome their trauma counseling will be provided. Similarly, counseling will be provided to parents before the child is repatriated.

Repatriation

Family is an indispensable institution for the full blossoming of children. Because, parental care, sibling affections are important for the healthy emotional and psychological growth of children. Short-stay homes are designed to offer only short-term rehabilitation. The services offered at the short-stay home cannot match the comprehensive role played by the family in ensuring the development of the child and is no way it can replace/substitute the important roles of family. Hence, unlike other NGOs, which are showing undue interest in retaining the children in their residential interest, the project will give utmost importance to repatriation, if that effort will not lead to further violence, abuse and exploitation.

Referral Services

Obviously, with a limited resource (both time and finance) the project cannot indulge in all sorts of activities. Hence, focusing more on the areas where other NGOs are not paying sufficient attention, the project will rely on other NGOs in which they have specialization and expertise. For instance, the project will rely on other NGOs to provide long-term residential care to abandoned children, rehabilitation of girl children and for specialized medical services.

Non-Formal Education

Education is a great socializing & empowering agent. There is no more powerful tool to protect and promote the rights of the child than education. There is no more effective opportunity available to street children than education to uplift themselves. Hence, the project will operate Non-formal Education centers at Contact centers, Drop-in-Shelter, Short-Stay Home and at street/working children prone areas. Numeracy, literacy, life-skills education, child rights education and personality development sessions will be provided to the children. If the children are interested in reviving their formal education, they will be admitted in Bridge courses and then in formal schools (either back home or in residential –institutions).

Transit School/Bridge Course

Survey revealed that, many children are running-away from home at certain level schooling after completing elementary education.

Hence, the project will operate Transit schools/Bridge courses at selected target slums in an effort to mainstream school-dropouts, street & working children and never-enrolled in to formal stream of education. Suitable child-friendly pedagogical methods will be followed in these centers.

Educational Background

Logistical Support for Formal Education

Deprivation of education & forced labor is also one of the causes for the incidence of street children. Hence, the project will provide logistical support to the children, who are mainstreamed into formal stream of education through transit/bridge schools. If the children are originating from neighboring district, and there is a likelihood of repatriation initiatives leading to obstruction of educational aspirations/pursuits, the project will repatriate the children in the first place and then help them to study in a residential school located in Vijayawada.

Vocational Skills Training

Suitable market relevant, remunerative vocational skills will be provided to children on the basis of their aptitude and aspirations.

Career Counseling & Apprenticeship, Job Placement Cell

On the completion of the Vocational training the project will provide career counseling to the children. Apprenticeship opportunity will be created and Job Placement Services will be provided to the children to enable them to become independent and self-reliant.

Entrepreneurship Skills Training/Consultancy Services/ Economic Development Assistance

For those children, who aspire to venture in to business world, Entrepreneurship development programs and consultancy services will be provided to identify viable sectors. Economic Development Assistance will be provided to children for start-up funds and equipment/assets.

Children's Savings Bank

Street children live day-by-day. They work from dawn to dusk to earn a meager amount and spend it immediately on cinema, alcohol, drugs, cigarettes and food, emerging empty-handed at the end of the day. There is no saving so no visions/aspirations for future.

Hence, the project will start an exclusive bank for children to enable them to save their hard-earned money and will encourage them to use it appropriately for their further development.

Establishing Commune Type of Living

For those grown-up children who cannot be repatriated for various reasons, the project will encourage them to live as a group and establish a commune type of living at appropriate places. This will help them to protect themselves from abuses of police and employers. Furthermore, it will also foster a sense of belonging and mutual-caring.

Self Help Groups & MED Assistance

The project will form Self-Help Groups for selected vulnerable families living in the target slums. Economic Development Assistance (EDA) will be provided to the members of these groups to enhance the capacity/resilience of their families.

Observance of Important Days

The project intends to organize campaigns in the run-up to Child Rights Day, Children's Day, Child Labor Day, Anti-Child Labor Day,

International AIDS Day, etc. to sensitize the street/working children and general public about these crucial issues.

Networking

The project will actively participate in the Forum for Child Rights and will strategically organize campaigns & combing-operations in association with these NGOs to rescue and rehabilitate street/working children.

Capacity Building for Staff

Working with street children requires special skills. Hence, the project will spend its considerable energy in building the capacity of the staff through trainings, exposure visits, etc. so as to enable them to handle the process deftly.

Family Strengthening Programs

Program services are directed towards families within the target group. Services are made available to the family as a whole, including all of the children and careers within the family.

Recommendation for Further Research

This present research is just a fore taste in the huge ocean of knowledge in the field of "Street Children." Much research is needed to rescue and rehabilitate these underprivileged children in our third world countries especially in India. The researchers' significant observation is that less research is done on the issue of successive rehabilitation work for street children. The readers must concentrate on the rehabilitation work especially to the street children.

Conclusion

'Street children' are a global phenomenon and it is a social disease that needs serious attention by the Christian community. It is an urban issue and a social sickness in our cities. These run away children are excluded from their homes, education, careers and even from the church because it seems that the church is not serious about them. The missiological research on children proves that this is the right age to help them to know God who can liberate them from all the oppressive structures. Street children should be concentrated on because the ages at which children run away from home and the ages at which children become Christians is almost the same. The church should also liberate street children who are oppressed, harassed, helpless and marginalized by the oppressive structures.

We also should ask ourselves:

Am I biased in excluding myself from the street children? Am I making a sound by dropping a coin in street kid's bowl or am I looking at him as an image of God who needs to be liberated from his/her oppressive struggles and structures? Why are they on the streets while the church is busy in worshipping Him in this nation? Are they important in the kingdom of God? Do we have a mission for them? How we can include these children into the families, society & the Church? What is my role in preventing, providing and protecting these street children that we often see on the streets or at the church gate?

References

1 Lima Soares and Zena de, "Children : A Permanent Challenge for the Churches," *International Review of Mission* 85, no. 338 (July 1996): 429.

2 Bryant Myers, "State of the World's Children : Critical Challenge to Christian Mission," *International Bulletin of Missionary Research* 18, no. 3 (July 1, 1994): 98.

3 "United Nations Development Programme (UNDP)" (Oxford University Press, New York, 1993), 24, http://hdr.undp.org/en/media/hdr_1993_en_chap2.pdf.

4 R. Agrawal, *Streetchildren: A Socio-Psychological Study* (Shipra Publications, 1999), 28.

5 Shanchobeni Yanthan and Pelekhono Zinyu, "Street Children and Christian Response," in *Children At Risk: Issues and Challenges* (Bangalore: ISPCK, 2009), 267.

6 John Boswell, *The Kindness of Strangers: The Abandonment of Children in Western Europe from Late Antiquity to the Renaissance* (University of Chicago Press, 1988), 172.

7 V. Chennupati et al., "Rehabilitation Programme for HIV/AIDS Afflicted Street Children in a District of South India," 1, accessed

September 25, 2014, http://www.iasociety.org/Abstracts/A9394.aspx.

8 "Street Children in India: Street Children Problem, an NGO Working for Indian Street Children," accessed September 25, 2014, http://i-indiaonline.com/sc_crisis_theproblem.htm.

9 Boswell, *The Kindness of Strangers*, 172.

10 Frampton F. Fox, "'Eating the Flesh of Our Sons and Daughters': Mission to Children-at-Risk through Parents Who Risk," *Missiology* 37, no. 4 (October 1, 2009): 501.

11 Yanthan and Zinyu, "Street Children and Christian Response," 271.

12 A. P. J. Abdul Kalam and Y. S. Rajan, *India 2020: A Vision for the New Millennium* (Penguin Books, 2002), 17.

13 Nitin Mehrotra, *Indian Retail Sector - A Primer* (ICFAI Books, 2007), vii.

14 "Majority of Street Children Face Sex Abuse in India," *The Times of India*, January 14, 2010, 1.

15 Marcel Lebrun, *Children in Crisis: Violence, Victims, and Victories* (R&L Education, 2011), 95.

16 Books LLC and General Books LLC, *Children's Street Culture: Urban Legend, Street Children, Hoop Rolling, Truce Term, Street Skateboarding, Skipping-Rope Rhyme, Bloody Mary* (General Books, 2010), 17.

17 Sarah Thomas de Benitez, "State of the World's Street Children: Research," *Consortium for Street Children: London*, 2011, 1–101.

18 Jayesh, "Street Children Essay," Social Issues, *Anti Essays*, (December 3, 2012), http://www.antiessays.com/free-essays/Street-Children-365355.html.

19 WORLD HEALTH ORGANIZATION, "A One-Way Street? Report on Phase I of the Street Children Project Part 3 of 9," Document, *WORLD HEALTH ORGANIZATION Programme on Substance Abuse*, (July 1993), 9, http://www.pangaea.org/street_children/world/who3.htm.

20 M. H. Abrams and Geoffrey Harpham, *A Glossary of Literary Terms* (Cengage Learning, 2014), 111.

21 Charles Dickens, *Selections from Household Words; a Weekly Journal* (New York: J. Miller, 1864), 335.

22 Jacob Riis, *How the Other Half Lives* (Applewood Books, 2011), 69.

23 *Child Labour: A Socio-Legal Perspective* (Pentagon Press, 2009), 85.

24 The United Nations Children's Fund, "State of the World's Children 2003," New York 2003, 37.
25 The United Nations Children's Fund, "The State of the World's Children 2006," New York 2006, 40–41.
26 Boswell, *The Kindness of Strangers*, 112.
27 WORLD HEALTH ORGANIZATION, "Street Children."
28 "Prevalence, Abuse & Exploitation of Street Children," accessed September 24, 2014, http://gvnet.com/streetchildren/India.htm.
29 ILO International Programme on the Elimination of Child Labour, *Every Child Counts: New Global Estimates on Child Labour* (ILO/IPEC, 2002), 26.
30 T. N. Kitchlu, *Exploited Child: A National Problem* (M.D. Publications Pvt. Ltd., 1996), 11.
31 Dawn Mission Trust, "Street Children in India - Children Education and Health," October 20, 2009, https://www.ammado.com/community/110475/articles/11741.
32 Duong Kim Hong and Kenichi Ohno, "Street Children in Vietnam: Interactions of Old and New Causes in a Growing Economy" (Vietnam Development Forum, July 2005), 6.
33 P. C. Sukla, ed., *Street Children and the Asphalt Life: Street Children and the Future Direction* (Delhi: Gyan Publishing House, 2005), 1.
34 P. Kilbourn, ed., *Street Children: A Guide to Effective Ministry* (MARC, 1997), 10.
35 Nandana Reddy, *Street Children of Bangalore: A Situational Analysis* (National Labour Institute, Child Labour Cell, 1992), 25.
36 http://gvnet.com/streetchildren/India.htm, 2011-03-20
37 "Street Children," 1.
38 T. J. Scanlon et al., "Street Children in Latin America," *British Medical Journal* 3 1 6, no. 23 (May 1998): 1596.
39 Scanlon et al., "Street Children in Latin America."
40 T. Scanlon, F. Scanlon, and Lamarao Nobre, *Working with Street Children*, vol. 3 (London: Taylor & Francis, 1993), 3.
41 Diversi M, Moraes N, and Morelli M, "New Directions for Child & Adolescent Development" (New York: Jossery Bass, 1999), 19–34.
42 Assefa Bekele and William E. Myers, *First Things First in Child Labour: Eliminating Work Detrimental to Children* (International Labour Organization, 1995), 6–7.
43 International Labor Organization, *Child Labour. Targeting the Intolerable. Report 86 VI (1)* (ILO/IPEC, 1998), 18.
44 Ibid., 22.

45 UNESCO, "Education for Street and Working Children in India" (Ministry of Human Resource Development, New Delhi, 2001), 22, Print.

46 Ibid., 23.

47 *Child Labour*, 90.

48 Alamgiri Kabir, "A Study on the Effectiveness of the Activities Taken for Street Children in Drop in Centers" (Dissertation, Master of Development, BRAC University, 2008), 18.

49 India Ministry of Social Justice and Empowerment, *Annual Report 1999-200: Ministry of Social Justice and Empowerment* (Delhi: Government of India, Ministry of Social Justice and Empowerment, 1999), 81.

50 Ibid., 85.

51 Kanchipuram Child Line, "Street Children," accessed September 26, 2014, https://sites.google.com/site/kanchipuramchildline/who-we-are.

52 Basavanthappa, *Community Health Nursing* (Jaypee Brothers Publishers, 2008), 363.

53 Scanlon et al., "Street Children in Latin America," 1596.

54 L Mishra, "Child Labour in India, Problems, Constraints and Challenges" (presented at the conference on Child Labor, Delhi: ILO/IPEC, 2000).

55 Ibid.

56 Care & Share, "Street Children," accessed September 26, 2014, http://www.careshareindia.org/streetkids.htm.

57 Helyar Mark, "Street Kids' Community Villages: Helping Homeless Children in India," accessed September 26, 2014, http://www.gonomad.com/2766-street-kids-community-villages-helping-homeless-children-in-india.

58 World Vision, "PROJECT DESIGN DOCUMENT: Vijayawada Street Children Project" (World Vision International, November 2008), 13.

59 Divakar, Interview given to P. V. Rao at World Vision office, Vijayawada, March 2, 2011.

60 http://www.careshareindia.org/streetkids.htm, 2011-03-21.

61 Interview with Mrs. Dhana Lakshmi at Vijayawada Bus station on 23rd Mar 2011.

62 World Vision, "PROJECT DESIGN DOCUMENT: Vijayawada Street Children Project."

Index

N

O

P

R

S

T

U

V

W